POWER
FOR
SALES PEOPLE

The Five Simple Steps of the Sales Process

POWER Quotes FOR

SALES PEOPLE

The Five Simple Steps of the Sales Process

Christopher J. Maloney

To order additional copies of this book, contact:
Xlibris Corporation
1-888-795-4274
www.Xlibris.com
Orders@Xlibris.com
54171

Contents

Author's Note to Readers 7

Introduction: Power Quotes for Sales People and
    The Five Simple Steps of the Sales Process..................................11

Step One*: Know Your Product and Define Your Market*

1. Read, Learn, Practice, Master your Craft
   and Know your Product! 15
2. Specialize, Target Marketing and Networking...........................25
3. Reputation, Character and Building Trust 31

Step Two: *Know Your Customer and Know Who is Buying*

4. The Golden Rule of Sales: Take Care of the Customer 43
5. Ask, Listen and Take Good Notes...47
6. Be Observant, Creative and Recognize Sales Opportunities.........57

Step Three: *Know How to Present Your Product and Market Yourself*

7. Prepare and Simplify Your Presentation......................................67
8. Present Your Product with Enthusiasm, Passion and Belief! 81
9. Smile, Laugh and Have a Pleasing Personality............................87
10. Ask for the Order . . . Again and Again and Again!......................93
11. Overcoming Objections and Rejection 97
12. Be Yourself and Use Your Personal Assets 101
13. Self Promotion, Advertising and Public Relations 107
14. Dress and Personal Appearance 113

Step Four: _Know Your Goals, Have a Plan and Take Action_

15. Think Big! 121
16. Goal Setting: Dream it, See it, Say it and Believe it! 125
17. Business Planning and Preparation 135
18. Discipline, Focus and Good Daily Habits 143
19. Time Management 149
20. Sales Leaders are Team Builders 157
21. Decide and Take Action Now! 165
22. Take Risks and Make Mistakes! 189

Step Five: _Know How to Stay Motivated and Enthusiastic_

23. The Success Focused Mind 203
24. Hard work, persistence, and a Never Die Attitude! 213
25. Overcoming Adversity and Getting Out of a Sales Slump 237
26. Top Sales People Embrace Change and Prosper 253
27. Health is Wealth 257
28. Reward Yourself Regularly and Often 263
29. The Winning Sales Attitude and Mindset! 269

Acknowledgements 283
About the Author 285

Author's Note to Readers

F OR OVER A quarter century I have had the privilege to sell with, hire, recruit, train and manage some of the highest producing commission sales people in the world. Many of these high achieving personalities have consistently out earned and made more in sales commissions and fees than many Fortune 500 CEOs. That's powerful!

In 2001, after the September 11th attacks on the World Trade Center, I was promoted to the position of National Sales Manager of a top-tier Wall Street Investment Banking firm. The firm was located in the shadows of the World Trade Center and our offices experienced severe damage. The firm, like many Wall Street firms, had a very difficult time communicating with their branch offices and sales people around the country. I was asked to travel to a number of our firm's branch offices to help stay in touch with our Account Executives that had become disjointed from their New York corporate headquarters. At one sales meeting that I was conducting in St. Louis, one of the biggest producers in the office raised his hand and interrupted, "Hey you're that Quote Guy in New York, right?" I responded, "Yeah, well, I guess I am." This multimillion dollar producer went on to say that he liked my daily sales notes on the stock and bond markets, but he really got the biggest charge out of the motivational quotes at the beginning and end of each daily sales note. He said, "Those simple little quotes are what really get my brain focused for the day. Forget the sales ideas and give me more of that stuff man. That's what I really need!"

On Wall Street or even in St. Louis, one comment does not make a trend. But then I heard it again in the next city and in fact, every branch that I traveled to. Here were some of the world's greatest, richest and most talented power brokers and industry sales leaders saying "Don't get me wrong pal, I like the sales notes, but man, I really love those quotes that pertain to selling and motivation." So many of the Account Executives would ask me, "Where do you find all those great sayings? You should put them in a book."

That was my "Ah Ha moment" in sales training and sales management. Even though for 20 years I had heard, read and practiced, ad nauseam, to K.I.S.S. or Keep It Stupid Simple, I never realized how simple the best of the best wanted their sales material and meetings to be. The Big Producer absolutely despises the long, drawn-out corporate meeting platform. If "time is money" then those long, boring sales meetings are burning the sales person's money. I have also learned that high achieving sales personalities receive, think, process and then present to their clients in brief, well structured and action-oriented sound bites. So why not reach the sales person in the same way? I realized that if you go long, you will always lose the best sales people; get your point across in a quick, well-worded *Power Quote* and you will reach and teach them every time.

Michel de Montaigne, the great Renaissance writer (and probably Shakespeare's sales coach) put it best, "I quote others in order to better express myself." And that is the basis of this short, but powerful sales training tool. A quote made by a great individual and used in the right learning situation is the purest and simplest communication method ever devised. *Power Quotes for Sales People and the Five Simple Steps of the Sales Process* cuts through hours of boring sales meetings and gets to the point in the quickest way. Rain Makers, Power Brokers and Top Producers don't have time for the long, drawn-out story. They want the guts of what the product or service will do so they can to get to the phones or out into their sales territory. They want quick sound bites—the bottom line!

A *Power Quote* is the shortest distance between teaching and understanding; between explaining and really getting it. Many a one line quote has even shaped the mettle of a nation and motivated countrymen to overcome tyranny. In September of 1779, with his ship listing and all but sunk by the British Fleet, Captain John Paul Jones responded back to the call for his surrender with the words, "I have not yet begun to fight!" His own shipmen, inspired by their Captain's resolve and determination, were instantly motivated by his seven simple words and ultimately turned the battle around and forced the opposing British captain to surrender his own ship to Captain Jones.

Power Quotes speak volumes in just a few words. Even corporate jingles become over-riding messages and direction for customers to act on and for employees and team mates to be motivated by. Who will ever forget the "Just Do it!" advertising campaign? The Nike Corporation literally did billions in sales while athletes and weekend warriors improved their own discipline by chanting their jingle. *Power Quotes* are clear, precise, thought provoking analogies that are delivered concisely to inform and inspire. *Power Quotes* create visuals in the mind. They are fireworks to the brain. *Power Quotes* also boil down how others have dealt with and overcome some of life's greatest hardships and challenges.

In my years of sales training and sales management of Financial Advisors and Account Executives on Wall Street, I also noticed that every high end sales training program from Xerox to Merrill Lynch and IBM all emphasize having a structured approach and organized program to the sales process. Plain and simply put, there is a sales path made up of logical and formulaic steps to closing sales and building a business. This, coupled with my "You're the Quote Guy" Ah Ha moment, I had the idea to simply plug in the greatest pearls of wisdom ever spoken into the formal structure and steps of the organized sales process.

Power Quotes for Sales People and the Five Simple Steps of the Sales Process is a sales training program that is essentially taught by some of the greatest people in history. What better way can there be to help motivate a sales person through a sales slump than to the thoughts, words and statements on overcoming adversity by say Sir Winston Churchill, Bob Marley or President John F. Kennedy? Ralph Waldo Emerson and Muhammad Ali have some of the strongest, most memorable pieces of advice on making your presentation short and to the point for the most desired outcome: getting your client to act now! Would you rather have "Corporate" leading you through a long and boring sales meeting on overcoming objections or perhaps Lance Armstrong and the great Roman philosopher Publilius Syrus? Big producers associate with greatness, especially in the sales training and motivational process. This is the sales process taught by history's most successful people.

There are countless numbers of general quote books, but no concise work exists that's geared towards and deals with the five key areas of the actual sales process. That's what *Power Quotes for Sales People* has done. These *Power Quotes* have been farmed, gathered and harvested from great works of literature, sports, business leaders, warriors, spiritual leaders, people who have overcome great hardships and tragedies, and from great salespeople themselves. As my Irish Grandmother used to say, "The shortest pencil is greater than the longest memory." So whenever I heard a pearl of wisdom roll off someone's tongue, I wrote it down so I could capture it forever. I have done this for years and now I have organized *Power Quotes for Sales People and the Five Simple Steps of the Sales Process* into an easy format and reference that applies to the structured sales process.

The goal of this book is simple: improve your selling skills and keep yourself motivated every day by employing any number of the philosophies offered up by history's greatest heroes and thinkers. Many of these *Power Quotes* may even spur you on to read and explore more about a specific individual that motivated and reached you through his or her spoken or written words. If the Power Brokers that I have been fortunate to have worked with found these Power Quotes helpful to their day, I know you will find yourself referring to *Power Quotes for Sales People and the Five Simple Steps of the Sales Process* for many years to come.

Lastly, if one well worded quote has positively changed the face, psyche and outcome of a nation, team, corporation or group of people in despair, just imagine what *Power Quotes for Sales People* can do for your selling career, personal income and net worth.

Introduction

Power Quotes for Sales People and
The Five Simple Steps of the Sales Process

L ET'S SIMPLIFY AND stay away from all complications. Sales and becoming successful in the greatest profession of all time is meant to be simple. You will now devote yourself to simplifying everything you do in the process and slowly, but surely, you will be breaking all of your company's records and reaching the goals you have set for yourself.

Anthony Robbins, the great motivational and success trainer said, "Success leaves clues." No simpler words have been spoken on the subject of life achievement. In fact, authors like Dale Carnegie and Napoleon Hill literally made a career and small fortune by studying those clues and respectively publishing the two greatest works of all time: *How to Win Friends and Influence People* and *Think and Grow Rich.* Studying those clues has created a multibillion dollar self-help and sales training industry. The one clue I have uncovered in my 25 years of financial sales, sales training and sales management is that the greatest sales people in any industry have the simplest selling style and approach. They make it look so easy that many of their coworkers and competitors are baffled in wonderment as to how they do it.

Stop wondering! If you really look for the clues as to why Big Producers are massively successful, you will find they simply have and follow a process and systematic sales path to closing sales, getting referrals and building a selling machine that is envied by all. They also have developed and worked at the skill to keeping themselves positive, enthusiastic and fired up!

Years ago, The Honda Corporation had a very simple ad campaign with the one word tag line: "*Simplify*". This campaign appealed to so many frazzled, uptight and stressed out car buyers who had so many options in their car purchasing decision. Honda's message was clear: Buy a Honda; it will simplify your life. And boy did Honda sell a ton of cars! Buyers want it simplified for them. They don't want too much meat on the sandwich if you know what I'm saying (Oops—another clear, concise saying that gets the point across quickly).

I promise not to bore you into a coma with pages and chapters and volumes and workbook exercises on the intricacies of the formalized sales path. No arrows to follow. No graphs to analyze and none of those annoying little side-bar "chat" boxes in the margins to distract you while you learn.

So let's get to it! The bottom line is there are really only five simple steps of the sales process: You have to know your product and define your market. You have to know your customer and know who is buying. You need to know how to present your product and market yourself. You have to know what your own goals are, have a plan and then take action towards reaching them. And lastly and perhaps most importantly, you must know how to constantly stay motivated and enthusiastic every single day of your selling life. That's it! That's all. It's not complicated and it's not rocket science. There is no secret. Don't fight it. Buy in and own it. It's that simple. The hardest part of learning how to sell is learning how to simplify. K.I.S.S. or Keep It Simple, Stupid must be your mantra. If you think there must be more to sales stardom, I'm glad you bought this book.

Power Quotes for Sales People is broken down into the Five Simple Steps of the Sales Process along with corresponding chapters that relate to each step and what you need to consider in order to close more sales. Each chapter will contain the greatest *Power Quotes* that relate and pertain to the skill set of that chapter. These *Power Quotes for Sales People* are thought provoking, inspirational, motivational and instructional. Most of all, they are there for you to get the point and improve your selling and closing skills in a simple and succinct way. Now that you know the Five Simple Steps of the Sales Process, let's start improving your skills by applying the simple and straight forward advice collected here and presented to you by some of the most exciting, successful and thought provoking people history has ever known.

Know Your Product and Define Your Market

Read, Learn, Practice, Master Your Craft and Know Your Product

Specialize, Target Marketing and Networking

Reputation, Character and Building Trust

Chapter 1

Read, Learn, Practice, Master your Craft and Know your Product!

Without training, they lacked knowledge.
Without knowledge, they lacked confidence.
Without confidence, they lacked victory.
Julius Caesar, Roman Emperor

Repeat anything often enough and it will start to become you.
Tom Hopkins, sales trainer and author

The secret of the man who is universally interesting is that he is universally interested.
William Dean Howells, author and critic

If you want to change someone, start with yourself first. From a purely selfish standpoint, it's a lot more profitable than trying to change and help others.
Dale Carnegie, success trainer and author

15% of one's financial success is due to one's technical knowledge and about 85% is due to skill in human engineering—to personality and ability to lead people.
Dale Carnegie, success trainer and author

The great aim of education is not knowledge, but action.
Dale Carnegie, success trainer and author

Education is the ability to meet life's situations.
Dale Carnegie, success trainer and author

The point to remember about selling things is that, as well as creating atmosphere and excitement around your products, you've got to know what you're selling.

Stuart Wilde, Metaphysical author

Your earning ability today is largely dependent upon your knowledge, skill and your ability to combine that knowledge and skill in such a way that you contribute value for which customers are going to pay.

Brian Tracy, sales trainer

The road to success is always under construction.

Brian Tracy, sales trainer

Those who do not study are only cattle dressed up in men's clothes.

Chinese proverb

You can learn a line from a win and a book from a defeat.

Paul Brown, football coach

Skill and confidence are an unconquered army.

George Herbert, Welsh poet

An idle mind is the devils workshop.

Irish proverb

I believe the brain is like a muscle; like any other it can be improved.

Ivan Lendl, tennis player

Books were my pass to personal freedom. I learned to read at age three, and soon discovered there was a whole world to conquer that went beyond our farm in Mississippi.

Oprah Winfrey, actor and media mogul

I knew there was a way out. I knew there was another kind of life because I had read about it. I knew there were other places, and there was another way of being.

Oprah Winfrey, actor and media mogul

A man's mind, stretched by a new idea, can never go back to its original dimension.

Oliver Wendell Holmes, Jr., U.S. Supreme Court Justice

The mind is like an elastic band; once stretched by a new idea, it never regains its original dimension.

Oliver Wendell Holmes, Jr., U.S. Supreme Court Justice

The next best thing to knowing something is knowing where to find it.

Samuel Johnson, writer

Spoon feeding in the long run teaches us nothing but the shape of the spoon.

E.M. Forster, writer

Education's purpose is to replace an empty mind with an open one.

Malcolm Forbes, magazine publisher

Know your enemy and know yourself; in a hundred battles you will never peril.

Sun Tzu, from *The Art of War*

If you are exposed to a concept, term, company, book, idea or comment three times in a relatively rapid succession, one should investigate and look into it to see if there is a need for deeper learning or change.

Beth Fisher, TCI Group

Repetition is the mother of skill.

Anthony Robbins, success trainer and author

Read the best books first or you may not have a chance to read them at all.

Henry David Thoreau, writer and philosopher

How many a man has dated a new era in his life from reading of a book.

Henry David Thoreau, writer and philosopher

After you've done a thing the same way for two years, look it over carefully. After five years, look at it with suspicion. And after ten years, throw it away and start all over.

Alfred Edward Perlman, railroad executive

Feed your head.

Grace Slick, Jefferson Starship

We are all, it seems, saving ourselves for the senior prom, but many of us forget that somewhere along the way we must learn to dance.

Alan Harrington, novelist

Growth itself contains the germ of happiness.

Pearl S. Buck, author and Nobel Prize Winner

New ideas can be good or bad—just the same as old ones.

U.S. President Franklin D. Roosevelt

The doors of wisdom are never shut.

Benjamin Franklin, statesman

If a man empties his purse into his head, no man can take it away from him. An investment in knowledge always pays the best interest.

Benjamin Franklin, statesman

He that won't be counseled can't be helped.

Benjamin Franklin, statesman

He who adds not to his learning diminishes it.

From The Talmud

Knowledge is power.

Francis Bacon, English philosopher and statesman

Action is the proper fruit of knowledge.

Thomas Fuller, M.D.

School is not the end, but only the beginning of an education.

U.S. President Calvin Coolidge

I have not met a man so ignorant that I couldn't learn something from him.

Galileo, astronomer

Employ your time in improving yourself by other men's writings so that you shall come easily by what others have labored hard for.

Socrates, Greek philosopher

Everyone thinks of changing the world, but no one thinks of changing himself.

Leo Tolstoy, author

It is what we think we know already that often prevents us from learning.

Claude Bernard, physiologist

I have never let my schooling interfere with my education.

Mark Twain, American writer

The man who does not read good books has no advantage over the man who can't read them.

Mark Twain, American writer

In the business world, everyone is paid in two coins: cash and experience. Take the experience first; the cash will come later.

Harold Geneen, businessman

Progress, far from consisting in change, depends on retentiveness. Those who cannot remember the past are condemned to repeat it.

George Santayana, writer and philosopher

Knowledge of what is possible is the beginning of happiness.

George Santayana, writer and philosopher

The wisest mind has something yet to learn.

George Santayana, writer and philosopher

The secret of business is to know something nobody else knows.

Aristotle Onassis, businessman

A bookstore is one of the only pieces of evidence we have that people are still thinking.

Jerry Seinfeld, comedian

Let us carefully observe those good qualities wherein our enemies excel us; and endeavour to excel them, by avoiding what is faulty, and imitating what is excellent in them.

Plutarch, Greek philosopher

The mind is not a vessel to be filled but a fire to be kindled.

Plutarch, Greek philosopher

I do not think much of a man who is not wiser today than he was yesterday.

U.S. President Abraham Lincoln

The brighter you are, the more you have to learn.

Don Herold, humorist and illustrator

Old men are always young enough to learn, with profit.

Aeschylus, Greek playwright

**He who knows not, and knows not that he knows not is a fool . . . shun him;
He who knows not, and knows that he knows not, is ignorant . . . teach him;
He who knows, and knows not that he knows, is asleep . . . awake him;
But he who knows, and knows that he knows, is a wise man . . . follow him.**

Ancient proverb

There's only one corner of the Universe you can be certain of improving, and that's your own self.

Aldous Huxley, writer

The important thing is not to stop questioning.

Albert Einstein, scientist

Imagination is more important than knowledge. For knowledge is limited, whereas imagination embraces the entire world, stimulating progress, giving birth to evolution.

Albert Einstein, scientist

Education is the movement from darkness to light.

> Allan Bloom, philosopher and academic

Only the educated are free.

> Epictetus, Greek Philosopher

The roots of education are bitter, but the fruit is sweet.

> Aristotle, Greek philosopher

A single conversation across the table with a wise man is better than ten years mere study of books.

> Henry Wadsworth Longfellow, writer

They know enough who know how to learn.

> Henry Adams, historian

To question a wise man is the beginning of wisdom.

> German proverb

There is no subject so old that something new cannot be said about it.

> Fyodor Dostoyevsky, Russian author

Knowledge is the antidote to fear.

> Ralph Waldo Emerson, philosopher

To the dull mind all nature is leaden. To the illumined mind the whole world burns and sparkles with light.

> Ralph Waldo Emerson, philosopher

Trust one who has gone through it.

> Virgil, Roman poet

In the beginning, I used to make one terrible play a game. Then I got so I'd make one a week and finally I'd pull a bad one about once a month. Now I'm trying to keep it down to one a season.

> Lou Gehrig, baseball player

Just when you think you've graduated from the school of experience, someone thinks up a new course.

Mary Waldrip, writer

One Accurate measurement is worth a thousand expert opinions.

Grace Murray Hopper—U.S. Navy Admiral

I like to stand in line, buy my popcorn and see a picture with the people.

Sherry Lansing, movie producer

If money is your hope for independence you will never have it. The only real security that a man will have in this world is a reserve of knowledge, experience and ability.

Henry Ford, automotive titan

A good head and a good heart are always a formidable combination.

Nelson Mandela, freedom fighter

Simply making consistent investments in our self-education and knowledge banks pays major dividends throughout our lives.

Jim Rohn, motivational writer

If we become increasingly humble about how little we know, we may be more eager to search.

John Templeton, investment professional

Knowledge learned the hard way combined with the avoidance of error, whenever and wherever possible, is the soundest basis for success in any endeavor.

Felix Dennis, magazine magnate

Education is a social process. Education is growth. Education is not a preparation for life; education is life itself.

John Dewey, philosopher

He who will not reason is a bigot; he who cannot is a fool; and he who does not is a slave.

William Drummond, Scottish scholar and philosopher

Write to be understood, speak to be heard, read to grow.

Lawrence Clark Powell, librarian and author

Good enough never is.

Debbi Fields, entrepreneur

It is better to learn late than never.

Publilius Syrus, Roman philosopher

Practice is the best of all instructors.

Publilius Syrus, Roman Philosopher

Better to be ignorant of a matter than to half know it.

Publilius Syrus, Roman writer

Each day is the scholar of yesterday.

Publilius Syrus, Roman philosopher

From the errors of others, a wise man corrects his own.

Publilius Syrus, Roman philosopher

The man who views the world at 50 the same as he did at 20 has wasted 30 years of his life.

Muhammad Ali, boxer

Many people who excel are self-taught.

Herb Ritts, photographer

I teach something called the Law of Probabilities, which says the more things you try, the more likely one of them will work. The more books you read, the more likely one of them will have an answer to a question that could solve the major problems of your life—make you wealthier, solve a health problem, whatever it might be.

Jack Canfield, author and success coach

I know that I am intelligent, because I know that I know nothing.

Socrates, Greek philosopher

No enemy is worse than bad advice.

Sophocles, Greek playwright

One learns by doing the thing; for though you think you know it, you have no certainty until you try.

Sophocles, Greek playwright

Whenever we're afraid, it's because we don't know enough. If we understood enough, we would never be afraid.

Earl Nightingale, motivational writer and author

Practice does not make perfect. Perfect practice makes perfect.

Vince Lombardi, football coach

Chapter 2

Specialize, Target Marketing and Networking

The secret of success is to know something nobody else knows.
Aristotle Onassis, shipping tycoon

People who know a lot about a little make more money than those who know a little about a lot.
Author unknown

He that is everywhere is nowhere.
Thomas Fuller, M.D.

Try to learn something about everything and everything about something.
Thomas Huxley, biologist

There is nothing worse than a brilliant image of a fuzzy concept.
Ansel Adams, photographer

Hay is more acceptable to an ass than gold.
Latin Proverb

The same man cannot well be skilled in everything; each has his special excellence.
Euripides, Greek playwright

Words calculated to catch everyone may catch no one.
Adlai Stevenson, politician and diplomat

A man who lives everywhere lives nowhere.
Marcus Valerias Martial, Latin poet

I don't know the key to success, but the key to failure is trying to please everybody.
> Bill Cosby, comedian

Blessed is he who has found his work; let him ask no other blessedness.
> Thomas Carlyle, Scottish writer

Please all and you will please none.
> Aesop's Fables

No one can play whatever position he chooses. If that happened in baseball, there'd be nine pitchers.
> Billy Martin, baseball coach

Every calling is great when greatly pursued.
> Oliver Wendell Holmes, Jr., Supreme Court Justice

Concentrate all your thoughts upon the work at hand. The sun's rays do not burn until brought to a focus.
> Alexander Graham Bell, inventor

Eye, stalk, chase, bite.
> A Sheppard discussing his Border Colley

Surround yourself with only people who are going to lift you higher.
> Oprah Winfrey, actor and media mogul

Always try to rub against money for if you rub against money long enough, some of it may rub off on you.
> Damon Runyon, newspaper man and author

It's not what you know, but who you know.
> An old powerbroker adage

To do two things at once is to do neither.
> Publilius Syrus, Roman philosopher

You cannot put the same shoe on every foot.
> Publilius Syrus, Roman philosopher

To take refuge with an inferior is to betray one's self.
Publilius Syrus, Roman philosopher

In marketing I've seen only one strategy that can't miss—and that is to market to your best customers first, your best prospects second and the rest of the world last.
John Romero, author

If you are going to be a successful duck hunter, you must go where the ducks are.
Bear Bryant, football coach

I cannot give you a formula for success, but I can give you the formula for failure which is: try to please everybody.
Herbert Bayard Swope, editor and journalist

Seek not every quality in one individual.
Confucius, philosopher

A straight path never leads anywhere except to the objective.
Andre Gide, French writer

Please all and you will please none.
Aesop Fables

All I know is, as long as I led the Southeastern Conference in scoring, my grades would be fine.
Sir Charles Barkley, professional basketball player

No man can serve two masters; for either he will hate the one and love the other; or he will hold to the one and despise the other.
Matthew 6:24

The perplexity of life arises from there being too many interesting things in it for us to be interested properly in any of them.
G. K. Chesterton, English journalist, philosopher and writer

He who serves two masters has to lie to one.
Portuguese proverb

Like associates with like.

> Cicero, Roman statesman

You can make more friends in two months by becoming interested in other people than you can in two years by trying to get other people interested in you.

> Dale Carnegie, success trainer and author

Necessity unites.

> German saying

Associate yourself with men of good quality if you esteem your own reputation. It is better be alone than in bad company.

> U.S. President George Washington

If you're not networking, you're "not working."

> Kevin Dyerly, financial advisor

When spider webs unite, they can tie up a lion.

> Ethiopian saying

The best time to make friends is before you need them.

> Ethel Barrymore, Academy Award winning actress

Dig your well before you're thirsty.

> Harvey Mackay, author and envelope magnate

Strangers are just friends who haven't met yet.

> Peter Rosen, business writer

Poverty, I realized, wasn't from only a lack of financial resources; it was isolation from the kind of people that could help you make more of yourself.

> Keith Ferrazzi, from *Never Eat Alone*

If a man does not make new acquaintance as he advances through life, he will soon find himself left alone.

> Samuel Johnson, English author

Go often to the house of thy friend; for weeds soon choke up the unused path.

Scandinavian Proverb

Be an opener of doors.

Ralph Waldo Emerson, philosopher

The ornament of a house is the friends who frequent it.

Ralph Waldo Emerson, philosopher

Friends are lost by calling often and calling seldom.

French saying

Even the weak become strong when they are united.

Johann Friedrich von Schiller

Don't ever slam a door; you might want to go back.

Don Herold, American humorist and writer

Friends and acquaintances are the surest passport to fortune.

Arthur Schopenhauer, German Philosopher

Cherish your human connections: your relationships with friends and family.

Barbara Bush, First Lady

Do not protect yourself by a fence, but rather by your friends.

Czech Proverb

I learned that we can do anything, but we can't do everything, at least not at the same time.

Dan Millman, athlete and motivational author

Chapter 3

Reputation, Character and Building Trust

Always do right; this will gratify some people and astonish the rest.
Mark Twain, American author

If you tell the truth you don't have to remember anything.
Mark Twain, American author

Seek not proud riches, but such as thou mayest get justly, use soberly, distribute cheerfully, and leave contentedly.
Francis Bacon, English philosopher and statesman

Associate yourself with men of good quality if you esteem your own reputation for it is better to be alone than in bad company.
U.S. President George Washington

All doors open to courtesy.
Thomas Fuller, M.D.

Character is much easier kept than recovered.
Thomas Paine, author

A good reputation is more valuable than money.
Publilius Syrus, Roman philosopher

What is left when honor is lost?
Publilius Syrus, Roman philosopher

God looks at the clean hands, not the full ones.
Publilius Syrus, Roman philosopher

He who has lost honor can lose nothing more.
Publilius Syrus, Roman philosopher

Always be a first-rate version of yourself.

Audrey Hepburn, actress

Reputation is what folks think you are. Personality is what you seem to be. Character is what you really are.

Alfred Armand Montapert, author and philosopher

Let no pleasure tempt thee, no profit allure thee, no ambition corrupt thee, no example sway thee, no persuasion move thee to do anything which thou knowest to be evil; so thou shalt live jollily for a good conscience is a continual Christmas.

Benjamin Franklin, Statesman

Glass, china and reputations are easily cracked and never mended well.

Benjamin Franklin, statesman

The time is always right to do the right thing.

Martin Luther King Jr., civil rights leader

Our lives begin to end the day we become silent about the things that matter.

Martin Luther King Jr., civil rights leader

Rather fall with honour than succeed by fraud.

Sophocles, Greek playwright

Honor is better than honors.

U.S. President Abraham Lincoln

You cannot escape the responsibility of tomorrow by evading it today.

U.S. President Abraham Lincoln

You can fool some of the people all of the time, and all of the people some of the time, but you can not fool all of the people all of the time.

U.S. President Abraham Lincoln

Modesty is the colour of virtue.

Diogenes, Greek philosopher

Character is long-standing habit.
Plutarch, Greek author

If all the world were just, there would be no need of valour.
Plutarch, Greek philosopher

You can't build a reputation on what you're going to do.
Henry Ford, automotive titan

Truth has no special time of its own. It hour is now—always.
Albert Schweitzer, surgeon and philosopher

Where is there dignity unless there is honesty?
Cicero, philosopher

Never esteem anything as of advantage to you that will make you break your word or lose your self-respect.
Marcus Aurelius Antonius, Roman Emperor

I try to do the right thing at the right time. They may just be little things, but usually they make the difference between winning and losing.
Kareem Abdul-Jabbar, basketball player

Sow an act and you reap a habit; sow a habit and you reap a character; sow a character and you reap a destiny.
George Dana Boardman, missionary

The best portion of a good man's life—his little nameless, unremembered acts of kindness and love.
William Wordsworth, poet

If you don't want anyone to know it, don't do it.
Chinese proverb

Those are my principles. If you don't like them I have others.
Groucho Marx, entertainer

The three hardest tasks in the world are neither physical feats nor intellectual achievements, but moral acts: To return love for hate, to include the excluded, and to say, "I was wrong."
Sydney J. Harris, writer

A great man shows his greatness by the way he treats little men.
Thomas Carlyle, Scottish writer

Motivate them, train them, care about them and make winners out of them. If we treat our employees correctly, they'll treat the customer's right. And if customers are treated right, they'll come back.
J.W. Marriott Jr., CEO of Marriott Hotels

Never let your sense of morals get in the way of doing what's right.
Isaac Asimov, science fiction writer

People have one thing in common; they are all different.
Robert Zend, Hungarian writer

Hard work spotlights the character of people: some turn up their sleeves, some turn up their noses and some don't turn up at all.
Sam Ewing, writer

Good will is the one and only asset that competition cannot undersell or destroy.
Marshall Field, retailer

Man is fond of counting his troubles, but he does not count his joys. If he counted them up as he ought to, he would see that every lot has enough happiness provided for it.
Fyodor Dostoyevsky, Russian author

Hold yourself responsible for a higher standard than anybody expects of you. Never excuse yourself.
Henry Ward Beecher, social reformer and abolitionist

Happiness is not the end of life, character is.
Henry Ward Beecher, social reformer and abolitionist

Watch your thoughts; they become words. Watch your words; they become actions. Watch your actions; they become habits. Watch your habits; they become character. Watch your character; it becomes your destiny.

> Anthony Robbins, Success trainer and author

Character is much easier kept than recovered.

> Thomas Paine, revolutionary and writer

I never give them hell. I just tell them the truth and they think it's hell.

> U.S. President Harry Truman

No man can climb out beyond the limitations of his own character.

> John Morley, British statesman

Nothing astonishes men so much as common sense and plain dealing.

> Ralph Waldo Emerson, philosopher

Common sense is as rare as genius.

> Ralph Waldo Emerson, philosopher

Who you are speaks so loudly I can't hear what you're saying.

> Ralph Waldo Emerson, philosopher

To believe in something and not to live it is dishonest.

> Mahatma Gandhi, statesman

It takes less time to do a thing right than to explain why you did it wrong.

> Henry Wadsworth Longfellow, writer and poet

You are not only responsible for what you say, but also for what you do not say.

> Martin Luther, religious reformist

Waste no more time arguing what a good man should be. Be one.

> Marcus Aurelius, Roman Emperor

An honest man's word is as good as his bond.

Cervantes, Spanish novelist and playwright

No legacy is so rich as honesty.

William Shakespeare, English poet and playwright

It's all right to be Goliath but always act like David.

Phil Knight, founder of Nike

Integrity can be neither lost nor concealed nor faked nor quenched nor artificially come by nor outlived nor I believe, in the long run, denied.

Eudora Wetley, writer

You cannot live a perfect day without doing something for someone who will never be able to repay you.

John Wooden, basketball coach

Ability may get you to the top, but it takes character to keep you there.

John Wooden, basketball coach

Be nice to people on your way up because you meet them on your way down.

Jimmy Durante, actor

Integrity is not a 90% thing or a 95% thing. Either you have it or you don't.

Peter Scotese, businessman

One of the greatest victories you can gain over someone is to beat him at politeness.

Josh Billings, humorist

It's the age-old struggle, the roar of the crowd on one side and the voice of your conscience on the other.

Douglas MacArthur, U.S. Army general

Character—the willingness to accept responsibility for one's own life—is the source from which self-respect springs.

Joan Didion, American journalist

Labor to keep alive in your breast that little spark of celestial fire called conscience.

U. S. President George Washington

To know what is right and not to do it is the worst cowardice.

Confucius, Chinese philosopher

The manner in which a man chooses to gamble indicates his character of lack of it.

William Saroyan, writer

There is no right way to do a wrong thing.

Turkish Proverb

The golden rule is of no use whatsoever unless you realize that it is your move.

Frank Crane, clergyman

Well done is better than well said.

Old English saying

It is our choices that show what we truly are, far more than our abilities.

J.K. Rowling, writer

Honesty is the first chapter in the book of wisdom.

U.S. President Thomas Jefferson

In some cases, walk away from business today, because that might affect your reputation, which will affect your ability to do business in a big way in the future.

Sandy Weill, billionaire financier

Civility costs nothing and buys everything.

Mary Wortley Montagu, writer

Rules cannot take the place of character.

Alan Greenspan, U.S. Federal Reserve Chairman

Success without honor is an unseasoned dish. It will satisfy your hunger, but it won't taste good.

Joe Paterno, football coach

My father taught me that reputation, not money, was the most important thing in the world.

William Rosenberg, founder of Dunkin' Donuts

A thousand words will not leave so deep an impression as one deed.

Henrik Ibsen, Norwegian playwright

I never deal with anyone except in one tongue, one policy and with one face.

Anwar Sadat, President of Egypt

It is no use walking anywhere to preach unless our walking is our preaching.

St. Francis of Assisi

A good name will shine forever.

Proverb

We should be careful and discriminating in all the advice we give. We should be especially careful in giving advice we wouldn't think of following ourselves.

Adlai Stevenson, politician and diplomat

The true test of character is not how much we know how to do, but how we behave when we don't know what to do.

John Holt, educator

The measure of a man's real character is what he would do if he knew he would never be found out.

Thomas Macaulay, British poet and politician

One man practicing sportsmanship is far better than fifty preaching it.

Knute Rockne, football coach

Integrity has no need of rules.

> Albert Camus, French author and philosopher

It takes 20 years to build a reputation and five minutes to ruin it. If you think about that, you'll do things differently.

> Warren Buffet, investor

Know Your Customer and Know Who is Buying

The Golden Rule of Sales: Take Care of the Customer

Ask Listen and Take Good Notes

Be Observant, Creative and Recognize Sales Opportunities

Chapter 4

The Golden Rule of Sales:
Take Care of the Customer

Do unto others as you would have them do unto you.
The Golden Rule

Treat every customer as if they sign your paycheck—because they do.
Author unknown

Take care of the customer or someone else will.
Author unknown

Do not to your neighbor what you would take ill from him.
Pittacus, Greek warrior

Avoid doing what you would blame others for doing.
Thales, Greek philosopher

What you wish your neighbors to be to you, such be also to them.
Sextus the Pythagorean

Do not do to others what would anger you if done to you by others.
Socrates, Greek philosopher

What thou avoidest suffering thyself seek not to impose on others.
Epictetus, Greek philosopher

Remember, the deepest principle of human nature is the craving to be appreciated.
William James, American psychologist and philosopher

Joint undertakings stand a better chance when they benefit both sides.

Euripides, Greek playwright

Quality is Job One!

Ford Motors corporate slogan

There is only one boss—The customer. And he can fire everybody in the company from the chairman on down, simply by spending his money somewhere else.

Sam Walton, founder of Wal-Mart

Take care of the customer and the customer will take care of you.

Author unknown

Dealing with people is probably the biggest problem you face, especially if you are in business. Yes, and that is also true if you are a housewife, architect or engineer.

Dale Carnegie, success trainer and author

When a customer enters my store, forget me. He is king

John Wanamaker, department store titan

Make a customer, not a sale.

Katherine Barchetti, retailer

Our greatest asset is the customer! Treat each customer as if they are the only one!

Laurice Leitao

Understanding human needs is half the job of meeting them.

Adlai Stevenson, politician and diplomat

All beautiful sentiments in the world weigh less than a single lovely action.

James Russell Lowell, poet and diplomat

If someone thinks they're being mistreated by us, they won't tell five people, they'll tell 5,000.

Jeff Bezos, Amazon.com

Customers provide you with the most accurate barometer of what's right and wrong.

> Herb Keller, founder of Southwest Airlines

If we don't take care of the customer, someone else will.

> An old sales maxim

There's a place in the world for any business that takes care of its customer after the sale.

> Harvey Mackay, author and envelope magnate

The Customer is King.

> Author unknown

The customer is the most important visitor on our premises. He is not dependent on us—we are dependent on him!

> Author unknown

Well done is better than well said.

> Benjamin Franklin, statesman

In business you get what you want by giving other people what they want.

> Alice MacDougall

Do what you do so well that they will want to see it again and bring their friends.

> Walt Disney, entertainment genius

There are no traffic jams along the extra mile.

> Roger Staubach, businessman and football player

This is the sum of all duty: do nothing to others which, if it were done to you, would cause you pain.

> Hindu saying

Do right. Do your best. Treat others as you want to be treated.

> Lou Holtz, football coach

They may forget what you said, but they will never forget how you made them feel.

Carl Buechner

Formula for success: under-promise and over-deliver.

Tom Peters, author

The most important persuasion tool you have in your entire arsenal is integrity.

Zig Ziglar, motivational writer

The game of life is a game of boomerangs. Our thoughts, deeds and words return to us sooner or later with outstanding accuracy.

Florence Schovel Shinn, writer

The only certain means of success is to render more and better service than is expected of you, no matter what your task may be.

Og Mandino, motivational author

It takes less time to do a thing right than to explain why you did it wrong.

Henry Wadsworth Longfellow, author and poet

Chapter 5

Ask, Listen and Take Good Notes

I keep six honest serving men. They taught me all I knew. Their names are What, and Why, and When and How and Where and Who.
> Rudyard Kipling, English writer and poet

Assumptions are the termites of relationships.
> Henry Winkler, actor

Assumption is the mother of all F#*@-ups!"
> Military saying

If A equals success, then the formula is A equals X plus Y and Z, with X being work, Y play, and Z keeping your mouth shut!
> Albert Einstein, scientist

Let the fool hold his tongue and he will pass for a sage.
> Publilius Syrus, Roman philosopher

I have often regretted my speech, never my silence.
> Publilius Syrus, Roman philosopher

I regret often that I have spoken; never that I have been silent.
> Publilius Syrus, Roman philosopher

Let a fool hold his tongue and he will pass for a sage.
> Publilius Syrus, Roman philosopher

I often regret that I have spoken; never that I have been silent.
> Publilius Syrus, Roman philosopher

Customers buy for their reasons, not yours.

Orvel Ray Wilson, author and speaker on sales and marketing

Listening, not imitation, may be the sincerest form of flattery.

Dr. Joyce Brothers, psychologist

A good listener is a silent flatterer.

An old Irish saying

Seek first to understand, then to be understood.

Ken Blanchard, PhD., author and management consultant

Feedback is the breakfast of champions.

Ken Blanchard, PhD., author and management consultant

Successful people ask better questions, and as a result, they get better answers.

Anthony Robbins, success trainer and author

He who asks is a fool for five minutes, but he who does not ask remains a fool forever.

Old Chinese saying

Listening is an attitude of the heart, a genuine desire to be with another which both attracts and heals.

J. Isham

If you spend more time asking appropriate questions rather than giving answers or opinions, your listening skills will increase.

Brian Koslow, businessman and entrepreneur

Everything has been said before, but since nobody listens we have to keep going back and beginning all over again.

Andre Gide, French writer

Speech is silver, but silence is golden.

French saying

Blessed is the man who, having nothing to say, abstains from giving in words evidence of the fact.
George Eliot, novelist

Nature has given men one tongue but two ears, that we may hear from others twice as much as we speak.
Epictetus, Greek philosopher

Good questions outrank easy answers.
Paul A. Samuelson, economist

Many attempts to communicate are nullified by saying too much.
Robert Greenleaf, author and management consultant

Learn to listen. Opportunity sometimes knocks very softly.
Jackson Brown, Jr., writer

Grieve not that men do not know you; grieve that you do not know men.
Confucius, Chinese philosopher

Assumption is the mother of mistakes.
Author unknown

It takes a great man to be a great listener.
U.S. President Calvin Coolidge

To listen is an effort, and just to hear is no merit. A duck hears also.
Igor Stravinsky, composer

It takes two to speak the truth: One to speak and another to hear.
Henry David Thoreau, writer and philosopher

The greatest compliment that was ever paid me was when someone asked me what I thought, and attended to my answer.
Henry David Thoreau, writer and philosopher

A wise old owl sat on an oak. The more he saw the less he spoke. The less he spoke the more he heard. Why aren't we like that wise old bird?
Author unknown

The most important thing in communication is to hear what isn't being saying.
> Peter Drucker, writer and management consultant

Give every man thy ear, but few thy voice.
> William Shakespeare, English poet and playwright

No matter how limited your vocabulary, it's big enough to let you say something you'll later regret.
> Adlai Stevenson, politician and diplomat

It is the province of knowledge to speak, and it is the privilege of wisdom to listen.
> Oliver Wendell Holmes, Jr., U.S. Supreme Court Justice

A gossip is one who talks to you about others; a bore is one who talks to you about himself; and a brilliant conversationalist is one who talks to you about yourself.
> Lisa Kirk, entertainer

I like to listen. I have learned a great deal from listening carefully. Most people never listen.
> Ernest Hemingway, writer

Courage is what it takes to stand up and speak; courage is also what it takes to sit down and listen.
> Sir Winston Churchill, British Prime Minister

Silence is a source of great strength.
> Lao Tzu, father of Taoism

Patience is the most necessary quality for business; many a man would rather you heard his story than grant his request.
> Lord Chesterfield, statesman and author

Drawing on my fine command of language—I said nothing.
> Robert C. Benchley, newspaper columnist and actor

Their silence is a loud cry.
> Cicero, Roman philosopher

Silence is more eloquent than words.
> Thomas Carlyle, Scottish Writer

There is only one rule for being a good talker—learn to listen.
> Christopher Morley, journalist and novelist

Sometimes you have to be silent to be heard.
> Stanislaw Lec, Polish poet

If you want people to think well of you, do not speak well of yourself.
> Blaise Pascal, French mathematician and philosopher

Do you wish people to believe good of you? Don't speak.
> Blaise Pascal, French mathematician and philosopher

Often silence is the wisest thing for a man to heed.
> Pindar, Greek poet

Silence is one of the great arts of conversation.
> Hannah More, English writer and philanthropist

To talk to someone who does not listen is enough to tense the devil.
> Pearl Bailey, author

There is no such thing as a worthless conversation, provided you know what to listen for. And questions are the breath of life for a conversation.
> James Nathan Miller, author

He who asks a question is a fool for five minutes; he who does not ask a question remains a fool forever.
> An old Chinese proverb

Listen or thy tongue will keep thee deaf.
> American Indian Proverb

Who speaks, sows; who listens, reaps.

Argentine proverb

We listen to what our customers wanted and acted on what they said. Good things happen when you pay attention.

John F. Smith, Jr., Chairman of General Motors

One often hears the remark, "He talks too much." But when did anyone hear the criticism, "He listens too much"?

Norman Augustine, executive

Be swift to hear, slow to speak, slow to wrath.

Bible, James 5:9

The art of conversation is the art of hearing as well as of being heard.

William Hazlitt, English writer

While the right to talk may be the beginning of freedom, the necessity of listening is what makes the right important.

Walter Lippmann, author

To listen closely and reply well is the highest perfection we are able to attain in the art of conversation.

Francois de La Rochefoucauld, French author

Sometimes listening itself may not be enough, some people must be prodded if you're to find out what they are thinking.

Mary Kay Ash, cosmetic company founder

The stillest tongue can be the truest friend.

Euripides, Greek playwright

Nothing is often a good thing to say and always a clever thing to say.

Will Durant, author

You can make more friends in two months by becoming interested in other people than you can in two years by trying to get other people interested in you.

Dale Carnegie, success trainer and author

Silence is as full of potential wisdom and wit as the unhewn marble of great sculpture.

Aldous Huxley, author

He who asks questions cannot avoid the answer.

Old proverb

Better ask twice than lose your way once.

Danish proverb

Silence is golden when you can't think of a good answer.

Muhammad Ali, boxer

Judge others by their questions rather than by their answers.

Voltaire, French philosopher

Listening is a magnetic and strange thing, a creative force. When we really listen to people there is an alternating current, and this recharges us so that we never get tired of each other. We are constantly being recreated.

Brenda Ueland, author

Where the river is deepest it makes the least noise.

Italian proverb

Keep quiet and people will think you a philosopher.

Latin proverb

Most of the successful people I've known are the ones who do more listening than talking.

Bernard Baruch, economist and presidential advisor

Better to remain silent and be thought a fool than to speak out and remove all doubt.

U.S. President Abraham Lincoln

Talk is cheap because supply exceeds demand.

Author unknown

There is no such thing as a worthless conversation, provided you know what to listen for. And questions are the breath of life for a conversation.
James Nathan Miller, author

Be a good listener. Your ears never get you in trouble.
Frank Tyger, writer

You can tell whether a man is clever by his answers. You can tell whether a man is wise by his questions.
Naguib Mahfouz, writer

Knowledge speaks, but wisdom listens.
Jimi Hendrix, musician

Listen or thy tongue will keep thee deaf.
Indian saying

The key is to get into the stores and listen.
Sam Walton, founder of Wal-Mart

The first duty of love is to listen.
Paul Tillich, philosopher

To listen well is as powerful a means of communication and influence as to talk well.
John Marshall, U.S. Supreme Court Justice

If you absolutely must speak in the selling process, make sure it's a question.
Chris Maloney

A good listener is not popular everywhere, but after a while, he gets to know something.
Wilson Mizner, playwright

I listened, motionless and still; and, as I mounted up the hill, the music in my heart I bore, long after it was heard no more.
William Wordsworth, poet

Listening is a magnetic and strange thing, a creative force. When we really listen to people there is an alternating current, and this recharges us so that we never get tired of each other. We are constantly being re-created.

Brenda Ueland, author

While the right to talk may be the beginning of freedom, the necessity of listening is what makes the right important.

Walter Lippmann, author

Listening is an attitude of the heart, a genuine desire to be with another which both attracts and heals.

J. Isham

The best time to hold your tongue is the time you feel you must say something or burst.

Josh Billings, humorist and writer

Many a men would rather you heard his story than grant his request.

Lord Chesterfield, British statesman

A major stimulant to creative thinking is focused questions. There is something about a well-worded question that often penetrates to the heart of the matter and triggers new ideas and insights.

Brian Tracy, sales trainer

Asking the right questions takes as much skill as giving the right answers.

Robert Half, businessman

You can tell whether a man is clever by his answers. You can tell whether a man is wise by his questions.

Naguib Mahfouz, Egyptian novelist

The most important thing in communication is to hear what isn't being said.

Peter F. Drucker, author and management consultant

My greatest strength as a consultant is to be ignorant and ask a few questions.

Peter F. Drucker, author and management consultant

We have two ears and one mouth so that we can listen twice as much as we speak.

Epictetus, Greek philosopher

It is wise to be silent when occasion requires.

Plutarch, Roman philosopher

Know how to listen, and you will profit even from those who talk badly.

Plutarch, Roman philosopher

Speak when you are angry and you will make the best speech you will ever regret.

Ambrose Bierce, writer

Supposing is good, but finding out is better.

Mark Twain, American author

Remember, a closed mouth gathers no foot.

Author unknown

It is right to give every man his due.

Plato, Roman philosopher

Millions saw the apple fall, but Newton was the one who asked why.

Bernard Baruch, financier

The shortest pencil is greater than the longest memory

An old Irish saying

Chapter 6

Be Observant, Creative and Recognize Sales Opportunities

The pessimist complains about the wind; the optimist expects it to change; the realist adjusts the sails.
William Arthur Ward, inspirational writer

If opportunity doesn't knock, build a door.
Milton Berle, comedian

Every adversity carries with it the seed of an equivalent or greater benefit.
Napoleon Hill, motivational writer

Scarcity builds clarity.
Sergey Brin, cofounder of Google

Buy your straw hats in the winter time.
Bernard Baruch, financier and Presidential advisor

A successful man is the one who had the chance and took it.
Roger Babson, business forecaster

Opportunity is missed by most people because it is dressed in overalls and looks like work.
Thomas A. Edison, inventor

Look and you will find it; what is unsought will go undetected.
Sophocles, Greek playwright

Luck is a sense to recognize an opportunity and the ability to take advantage of it.
Samuel Goldwyn, Academy Award winner, producer

When one door closes, another door opens, but we so often look so long and so regretfully upon the closed door that we do not see the ones which open for us.

Alexander Graham Bell, inventor

Know thine opportunity.

Pittacus, Greek warrior and sage

An essential aspect of creativity is not being afraid to fail.

Andre Agassi, tennis player

While we stop to think, we often miss our opportunity.

Publilius Syrus, Roman philosopher

The opportunity is often lost by deliberating.

Publilius Syrus, Roman philosopher

For all the days prepare and meet them all alike: When you are the anvil, bear. When you are the hammer, strike!

Edwin Markham, American poet

In great affairs we ought to apply ourselves less to creating chances than to profiting from those that offer.

La Rochefoucauld, French writer

Men talk about bible miracles because there is no miracle in their lives. Cease to gnaw that crust! There is ripe fruit over your head.

Henry David Thoreau, writer and philosopher

Frankly, I think it pisses God off if you walk by the color purple in a field somewhere and don't notice it.

Alice Walker, author of *The Color Purple*

The aim of life is to live and to live means to be aware, joyously, drunkenly, serenely, divinely aware.

Henry Miller, author and painter

Be a football to time and chance. The more kicks the better so you can inspect the whole game and know its utmost law.

Ralph Waldo Emerson, philosopher

Asking "What if" questions are not only a lot of fun, it also gives you the freedom to think along different lines.

Roger Von Oech, creativity coach

There is no security on this earth; there is only opportunity.

U.S. General Douglas MacArthur

The level of our success is limited only by our imagination and no act of kindness, however small, is ever wasted.

Aesop, Greek philosopher

When written in Chinese, the word "crisis" is composed of two characters: one represents danger and the other represents opportunity.

U.S. President John F. Kennedy

I dance to the tune that is played.

Spanish proverb

There is no bear market for good ideas.

Financial Services advertisement slogan

Some men go through a forest and see no firewood.

Old English saying

Too many people miss the silver lining because they are expecting gold.

Maurice Setter

You can't use up creativity. The more you use, the more you have.

Maya Angelou, poet

Opportunities are often things you haven't noticed the first time around.

Catherine Deneuve, actress

Genius means little more than the ability to perceive in an unhabitual way.

William James, psychologist

Common sense is not so common.

Voltaire, French philosopher

If everyone is thinking alike, then somebody isn't thinking.

U.S. General George S. Patton

More gold has been mined from the thoughts of men than has ever been taken from the earth.

Napoleon Hill, motivational writer

All truths are easy to understand once they are discovered; the point is to discover them.

Galileo, astronomer and inventor

It takes a very unusual mind to undertake the analysis of the obvious.

Alfred North Whitehead, mathematician and philosopher

The best place to hide anything is in plain view.

Edgar Allan Poe, writer and poet

Minds are like parachutes; they work best when open.

Sir Thomas Robert Dewar, Scotch Whiskey distiller

The empires of the future are the empires of the mind.

Sir Winston Churchill, British Prime Minister

The pessimist sees difficulty in every opportunity. The optimist sees opportunity in every difficulty.

Sir Winston Churchill, British Prime Minister

Too many people overvalue what they are not and undervalue what they are.

Malcolm Forbes, Magazine publisher

I skate to where the puck is going to be, not where

Wayne Gretzky, hockey player

**To achieve the impossible, one must think the absul
everyone else has looked, but to see what no one els**

Author unknown

**Nowadays some people expect the door of opportunity to be opened
by remote control.**

M. Charles Wheeler

**Creative minds have always been known to survive any kind of bad
training.**

Anna Freud, psychoanalyst

**Any activity becomes creative when the doer cares about doing it
right or doing it better.**

John Updike, writer

You can't see the future through a rearview mirror.

Peter Lynch, investor

A strong imagination begetteth opportunity.

Michel de Montaigne, French Renaissance writer

**The cleverly expressed opposite of any generally accepted idea is
worth a fortune to somebody.**

Francis Scott Key Fitzgerald, writer

A wise man will make more opportunities than he finds.

Francis Bacon, English philosopher and statesman

Some folk want their luck buttered.

Thomas Hardy, English novelist

In the middle of difficulty lies opportunity.

Albert Einstein, scientist

gence is quickness in seeing things as they are.
George Santayana, philosopher

The best thing that ever happened to me was not having money when I started my company—it forced me to be creative.
Robert Stevens, founder of the Geek Squad

Luck is preparation multiplied by opportunity.
Seneca, Roman Philosopher

I always tried to turn every disaster into an opportunity.
John D. Rockefeller, Jr., oil magnate

Opportunity often comes disguised in the form of misfortune or temporary defeat.
Napoleon Hill, motivational writer

There is no security on this earth, there is only opportunity.
U.S. General Douglas MacArthur

If you view all the things that happen to you, both good and bad, as opportunities, then you operate out of a higher level of consciousness.
Les Brown, motivational speaker

Opportunities? They are all around us. There is power living latent everywhere waiting for the observant eye to discover it.
Orison Swett Marden, writer

Small opportunities are often the beginning of great enterprises.
Demosthenes, Greek Statesman

The ladder of success is best climbed by stepping on the rungs of opportunity.
Ayn Rand, author

The hardest thing in life is to learn which bridge to cross and which to burn.
Laurence Peter, author of *the Peter Principle*

Customers buy for their reasons, not yours
> Orvel Ray Wilson, motivational speaker and writer

Opportunity dances with those on the dance floor.
> Russian proverb

If a window of opportunity appears, don't pull down the shade.
> Tom Peters, author

I can't understand why people are frightened of new ideas. I'm frightened of the old ones.
> John Milton Cage, Jr., composer

The best way to have a good idea is to have lots of ideas.
> Linus Pauling, scientist

Half our mistakes in life arise from feeling when we ought to think, and thinking when we ought to feel.
> John Churton Collins, writer

Great moments are born from great opportunities.
> Herb Brooks, hockey coach

We are continually faced by great opportunities brilliantly disguised as insoluble problems.
> Lee Iacocca, automotive executive

The man who has no imagination has no wings.
> Muhammad Ali, boxer

Readiness is all.
> William Shakespeare, English poet and playwright

Trust your hunches. They're usually based on facts filed away just below the conscious level.
> Dr. Joyce Brothers, psychologist and advice columnist

Opportunities are seldom labeled.
> John Shedd, writer

The two worst strategic mistakes to make are acting prematurely and letting an opportunity slip; to avoid this, the warrior treats each situation as if it were unique and never resorts to formulae, recipes or other people's opinion.

Paul Coelho, author

Know How to Present Your Product and Market Yourself

Prepare and Simplify Your Presentation

Present Your Product with Enthusiasm, Passion and Belief

Smile, Laugh and Have a Pleasing Personality

Ask for the Order . . . again and again and again!

Overcoming Objections and Rejection

Be Yourself and Use Your Personal Assets

Self Promotion, Advertising and Public Relations

Dress and Personal Appearance

Chapter 7

Prepare and Simplify Your Presentation

K.I.S.S. Keep It Simple, Stupid.
Keep It Short and Sweet.
Keep It Short and Simple
Old sales maxim

A good salesman can take ten facts about a product and by stressing some and de-emphasizing others create ten different impressions. That's what salesmanship really is: positioning the facts to get the desired response.
Mark McCormack, The father of Sports Management

Less is more.
Ludwig Mies van der Rohe, architect

When I get ready to talk to people, I spend two thirds of the time thinking what they want to hear and one third thinking about what I want to say.
U.S. President Abraham Lincoln

Give me six hours to chop down a tree and I will spend the first four sharpening the axe.
U.S. President Abraham Lincoln

Up is good. Down is bad.
Ralph Acampora, stock market technician

Do not say a little in many words but a great deal in a few.
Pythagoras, Greek philosopher

Simplicity is the ultimate sophistication.
Leonardo Da Vinci, Scientist

A short saying oft contains much wisdom.
> Sophocles, Greek playwright

Beauty of style and harmony and grace and good rhythm depend on simplicity.
> Plato, Greek philosopher

Persuasion is often more effectual than force.
> Aesop, Greek philosopher

Words are, of course, the most powerful drug used by mankind.
> Rudyard Kipling, English author and poet

Saying nothing sometimes says the most.
> Emily Dickinson, writer and poet

Omit needless words.
> William Strunk Jr., author of *the Elements of Style*

The more you know, the less you need to say.
> Jim Rohn, motivational writer

I have never been hurt by what I have not said.
> U.S. President Calvin Coolidge

Much silence makes a powerful noise.
> African saying

I tell you and you forget. I show you and you remember. I involve you and you understand.
> Eric Butterwort

Never talk away the magic.
> Old Danish Saying

If you talk to a man in a language he understands, that goes to his head. If you talk to him in his language, that goes to his heart.
> Nelson Mandela, African statesman and freedom fighter

Many a time the thing left silent makes for happiness.

Pindar, Greek poet

Great deeds give choice of many tales. Choose a slight tale, enrich it large, and then let wise men listen.

Pindar, Greek poet

A thing said walks in immortality if it has been said well.

Pindar, Greek poet

Everyone hears only what he understands.

Johann Wolfgang von Goethe, German playwright

A recent publication on the marketing of cabbage contains, according to one report, 26,941 words. It is noteworthy in this regard that the Gettysburg Address contains a mere 279 words while the Lord's Prayer comprises but 67.

Norman R. Augustine, aircraft businessman

Let thy speech be short, comprehending much in few word; be as one that knoweth and yet holdeth his tongue.

From *The Book of Sirach*

Our life is frittered away by detail. Simplify, simplify!

Henry David Thoreau, writer and philosopher

If it takes a lot of words to say what you have in mind, give it more thought.

Dennis Roth, author

Do not say a little in many words, but a great deal in a few.

Pythagoras, mathematician

Men who know little say much. Men who know much say little.

Author unknown

Well timed silence is the most commanding expression.

Mark Helprin, novelist

The more you say, the less people remember.
Anatole France, author

Chance favors the prepared mind.
Louis Pasteur, scientist

Winning can be defined as the science of being totally prepared.
George Allen, football coach

He who knows does not speak. He who speaks does not know.
Lao Tzu, founder of Taoism

The notes I handle no better than many pianists. But the pauses between the notes, ah, that is where the art resides.
Arthur Schnabel, classical pianist

Human beings are creatures of emotion, not creatures of logic. They are motivated by fear, greed, pride, vanity, prejudices and sex.
Dale Carnegie, success trainer and author

Begin with something interesting in your first sentence. Not the second. Not the third. The first! F-I-R-S-T-! First.
Dale Carnegie, success trainer and author

There are four ways and only four ways in which we have contact with the world. We are evaluated and classified by these four contacts: what we do, how we look, what we say and how we say it.
Dale Carnegie, success trainer and author

Say what you mean and mean what you say.
U.S. General George S. Patton

The right word may be effective, but no word was ever effective as a rightly timed pause.
Mark Twain, American author

Noise proves nothing. Often a hen who has merely laid an egg cackles as if she had laid an asteroid.
Mark Twain, American author

A powerful agent is the right word. Whenever we come upon one of those intensely right words in a book or newspaper the resulting effect is physical as well as spiritual and electrically prompt.

Mark Twain, American author

Pleasing ware is half sold.

George Herbert, Welsh poet and orator

Abuse of words has been the greatest instrument of sophistry and chicanery, of party, faction, and divisions of society.

U.S. President John Adams

The best cause requires a good pleader.

Dutch proverb

Good communication is stimulating as black coffee and just as hard to sleep after.

Anne Morrow Lindbergh

How forcible are right words

Bible, Job 6: 25

Perfection is achieved not when there is nothing more to add, but when there is nothing left to take away.

Antoine de Saint-Exupery, writer

You can't believe how hard it is for people to be simple, how much they fear being simple. They worry that if they're simple, people will think they're simple-minded. In reality, of course, it's just the reverse: Clear, tough minded people are the most simple.

Jack Welch, CEO of General Electric

Every idea you present must be something you could get across easily at a cocktail party with strangers.

Jack Welch, CEO of General Electric

Simple messages travel faster, simpler designs reach the market faster, and the elimination of clutter allows faster decision-making.

Jack Welch, CEO of General Electric

Brevity is the soul of lingerie.
>   Dorothy Parker, writer

Nothing astonishes men so much as common sense and plain dealing.
>   Ralph Waldo Emerson, philosopher

Put the argument into a concrete shape, into an image, some hard phrase, round and solid as a ball, which they can see and handle and carry home with them and the cause is half won.
>   Ralph Waldo Emerson, philosopher

If a man will kick a fact out of the window, when he comes back he finds it again in the chimney corner.
>   Ralph Waldo Emerson, philosopher

Too many pieces of music finish too long after the end.
>   Igor Stravinsky, Russian composer

If it were better, it wouldn't be as good.
>   Brendan Gill, on the play Butterflies are Free

The cunning old codger knows that no emphasis often constitutes the most powerful emphasis of all.
>   Cleath Brooks, On Robert Frost

It is much easier to write a long book than a short one.
>   I.M. Wise, educator and rabbi

Silence is one of the hardest arguments to refute.
>   Josh Billings, humorist

The author should shut his mouth when his work begins to speak.
>   Friedrich Nietzsche, German philosopher

Let thy speech be short, comprehending much in few words.
>   Apocrypha

The visual image created should speak for itself.
> Trevor Chamberlain, painter

To be brief is almost a condition of being inspired,
> George Santayana, writer and philosopher

When your work speaks for itself, don't interrupt.
> Henry J. Kaiser, industrialist

When your work speaks for itself, don't interrupt.
> Henry J. Kaiser, industrialist

Harp not on that string.
> William Shakespeare, English poet and playwright

Men of few words are the best of men.
> William Shakespeare, English poet and playwright

Have more than thou showest, speak less than thou knowest.
> William Shakespeare, English poet and playwright

Love's best habit is a soothing tongue.
> William Shakespeare, English poet and playwright

Mend your speech a little, lest it may mar your fortunes.
> William Shakespeare, English poet and playwright

The silence often of pure innocence persuades when speaking fails.
> William Shakespeare, English poet and playwright

All pleasantry should be short and it might even be as well were the serious short also.
> Voltaire, French writer and philosopher

Well timed silence hath more eloquence than speech.
> Martin Farquhar Tupper, English writer

It's not the will to win that matters, everyone has that. It's the will to prepare to win that matters.

Bear Bryant, football coach

Perfect simplicity is unconsciously audacious.

George Meredith, author

Simplicity, simplicity, simplicity! I say let your affairs be two or three and not a hundred or a thousand; instead of a million count half a dozen and keep your accounts on your thumb-nail.

Henry David Thoreau, writer and philosopher

Our life is frittered away by detail . . . Simplify, simplify.

Henry David Thoreau, writer and philosopher

I don't say everything, but I paint everything.

Pablo Picasso, artist

The art of art, the glory of expression and the sunshine of the light of letters is simplicity.

Walt Whitman, writer

When you are at sea, keep clear of land.

Publilius Syrus, Roman philosopher

Speech is a mirror of the soul; as a man speaks, so he is.

Publilius Syrus, Roman philosopher

The most valuable of all talents is that of never using two words when one will do.

U.S. President Thomas Jefferson

Simplify and add lightness.

Colin Chapman, founder of Lotus

If you want them to show you the money, you better show them the reason.

Harvey Mackay, envelope salesman

Tell them quick. Tell them often.
>William Wrigley Jr., chewing gum industrialist

In bating a mouse trap with cheese, always leave room for the mouse.
>Saki, British writer

The exact words you use are far less important than the energy, intensity and conviction with which you use them.
>Author unknown

The secret to succeeding in a competitive business is to take something that's common and make it uncommon.
>John D. Rockefeller, Jr., oil magnate

Words can sometimes, in moments of grace, attain the quality of deeds.
>Elie Wiesel, journalist and Holocaust survivor

The road to the heart is the ear.
>Voltaire, French writer and philosopher

In real estate, it's location, location, location. In business, it's differentiate, differentiate, differentiate.
>Roberto Goizueta, beverage executive

Nobody reads advertising. People read what interests them.
>Howard Gossage, advertising executive

The ability to express an idea is as important as the idea itself.
>Bernard Baruch, financier and presidential advisor

The man who makes a bad 30-minute speech to 200 people wastes only a half hour of his own time, but he wastes 100 hours of the audience's time—which should be a hanging offense.
>Jenkin Lloyd Jones, newspaper publisher

Things seen are mightier than things heard.
>Alfred Lord Tennyson, English poet

If you have an important point to make, don't try to be subtle or clever. Use a pile driver. Hit the point once. Then come back and hit it again. Then hit it a third time—a tremendous whack!

Sir Winston Churchill, British Prime Minister

If you have knowledge, let others light their candles with it.

Sir Winston Churchill, British Prime Minister

We always weaken whatever we exaggerate.

Jean-Francois De La Harpe, French playwright

The most perfect technique is that which is not noticed at all.

Pablo Casals, cellist

The artist must say it without saying it.

Duke Ellington, jazz musician

To be believed, make the truth unbelievable.

Napoleon Bonaparte, French military and political leader

We create our menus by starting with an inventory of what looks good in the garden.

Sabrina Schiller, restaurateur

Ours is the country where in order to sell your product, you don't so much point out its merits as you first work like hell to sell yourself.

Louis Kronenberger, critic and writer

You can say the right thing about a product and nobody will listen. You've got to say it in such a way that people will feel it in their gut. If they don't feel it, nothing will happen.

William Bernbach, advertising executive

Ask yourself, did it catch my attention, hold my interest, pierce my armor, speak English, center on me and make a point?

Allen Kay, advertising executive

Those whose cause is just will never lack good arguments.

Euripides, Greek playwright

In a just cause, the weak will beat the strong,
Sophocles, Greek playwright

It is always the latest song that an audience applauds the most.
Homer, from the Odyssey

He that has no silver in his purse should have silver on his tongue.
Thomas Fuller, M.D.

True eloquence consists in saying all that should be said, and that only.
La Rochefoucauld, French author

Life is like a play: it's not the length, but the excellence of the acting that matters.
Seneca, Roman philosopher

What is required is not a lot of words, but effectual ones.
Seneca, Roman philosopher

A wise man recognizes the convenience of a general statement, but he bows to the authority of a particular fact.
Oliver Wendell Holmes, Jr., U.S. Supreme Court Justice

You can have brilliant ideas, but if you can't get them across, your ideas won't get you anywhere.
Lee Iacocca, automotive executive

Let no one say that I have said nothing new; the arrangement of the subject is new.
Pascal, French philosopher

Tact is the knack of making a point without making an enemy.
Isaac Newton, scientist

We are cups, constantly and quietly being filled. The trick is knowing how to tip ourselves and let the beautiful stuff out.
Ray Bradbury, author

Less is more and usually comes a lot cheaper.
Richard Templar, author

I run on the road, long before I dance under the lights.
Muhammad Ali, boxer

If the timing isn't right, it doesn't matter how terrific your ideas are or how well you present a case.
Stuart Levine, from *Cut to the Chase*

In the factory we make cosmetics; in the drugstore we sell hope.
Charles Revson, cosmetic industrialist

If you're trying to persuade people to do something, or buy something, it seems to me you should use their language, the language in which they think.
David Ogilvy, advertising executive

What helps people helps business.
Leo Burnett, advertising executive

If you are writing about baloney, don't try to make it Cornish Hen, because that is the worst kind of baloney there is. Just make it darned good baloney.
Leo Burnett, advertising executive

Good teaching is one-fourth preparation and Three-fourths Theater.
Gail Godwin, novelist

Man who know little say much. Man who know much say little.
Author unknown

I quote others in order to better express myself.
Michel de Montaigne, French writer

The most valuable of all talents is that of never using two words when one will do.
U.S. President Thomas Jefferson

If you can't explain it simply, you don't understand it well enough.

Albert Einstein, scientist

Good things, when short, are twice as good.

Tom Stoppard, playwright

Many attempts to communicate are nullified by saying too much.

Robert Greenleaf, management consultant

There are tones of voice that mean more than words.

Robert Frost, poet

If you are writing about baloney, don't try to make it a Cornish hen because that is the worst kind of baloney there is. Just make it darned good baloney.

Leo Burnett, advertising executive

Good communication is as stimulating as black coffee, and just as hard to sleep after.

Anne Morrow Lindbergh, author

Fast is fine, but accuracy is everything.

Xenophon, Greek warrior

Do not say a little in many words, but a great deal in a few.

Pythagoras, philosopher

Imagination is the highest kite one can fly.

Lauren Bacall, actress

You can have brilliant ideas, but if you can't get them across, your ideas won't get you anywhere.

Lee Iacocca, automotive titan

Tell me and I'll forget. Show me and I'll remember. Involve me and I'll understand.

Confucius, Chinese philosopher

Proper words in proper places make the true definition of style.

Jonathan Swift, writer and playwright

The finest language is mostly made up of simple, unimposing words.

George Eliot, writer

Speak properly, and in as few words as you can, but always plainly; for the end of speech is not ostentation, but to be understood.

William Penn, founder of Pennsylvania

Remember not only to say the right thing in the right place, but far more difficult still, to leave unsaid the wrong thing at the tempting moment.

Benjamin Franklin, statesman

Making the simple complicated is commonplace; making the complicated simple, awesomely simple, that's creativity.

Charles Mingus, jazz musician

Every creative act requires elimination and simplification. Simplification results from a realization of what's essential.

Hans Hoffman, artist

The ability to simplify means to eliminate the unnecessary so that the necessary may speak.

Hans Hoffman, artist

It should be possible to explain the laws of physics to a barmaid.

Albert Einstein, scientist

It's taken me all my life to learn what not to play.

Dizzy Gillespie, musician and bandleader

I have a "play the melody" philosophy. It means don't over arrange. Don't make life difficult. Just play the melody and do it the simplest way possible.

Jackie Gleason, Actor and comedian

Chapter 8

Present Your Product with Enthusiasm, Passion and Belief!

Enthusiasm moves the world.
> Arthur James Balfour, British Prime Minister

You must stir it and stump it and blow your own trumpet or trust me, you haven't a chance.
> W.S. Gilbert, English playwright

Without passion you don't have energy, without energy you have nothing.
> Donald Trump, real estate magnate

People are persuaded more by the depth of your conviction than by the height of your logic.
> Cavett Robert, founder of *the National Speakers Association*

Catch on fire with enthusiasm and people will come for miles to watch you burn.
> John Wesley, English clergyman

None are so old as those who have outlived enthusiasm.
> Henry David Thoreau, author and philosopher

Act enthusiastic and you become enthusiastic.
> Dale Carnegie, success trainer and author

Men, as well as women, are much oftener led by their hearts than by their understandings.
> Lord Chesterfield, British statesman

The exact words you use are far less important than the energy, intensity and conviction with which you use them.

Jules Rose

Nothing great was ever achieved without enthusiasm.

Ralph Waldo Emerson, philosopher

Enthusiasm is the mother of effort and without it nothing great was ever achieved.

Ralph Waldo Emerson, philosopher

There is no strong performance without a little fanaticism in the performer.

Ralph Waldo Emerson, philosopher

Every great and commanding movement in the annals of the world is the triumph of enthusiasm.

Ralph Waldo Emerson, philosopher

Knowledge is power, but enthusiasm pulls the switch.

Ivern Ball, poet

If you can give your son or daughter only one gift, let it be enthusiasm!

Bruce Barton, advertising executive and U.S. Congressman

No tears in the writer, no tears in the reader. No surprise in the writer, no surprise in the reader.

Robert Frost, author

If you aren't fired with enthusiasm, you'll be fired with enthusiasm.

Vince Lombardi, football coach

You can't sweep other people off their feet if you can't be swept off your own.

Clarence Day, author

Experience shows that success is due less to ability than to zeal.

Charles Buxton, British statesman

Get excited and enthusiastic about your own dream. This excitement is like a forest fire—you can smell it, taste it and see it a mile away.

Denis Waitley, sales trainer

One person with passion is better than 40 people merely interested.

E.M. Forster, English novelist

Reason will always be the slave of passion.

Plato, Greek philosopher

I studied the lives of great men and famous women and I found that the men and women who got to the top were those who did the jobs they had in hand, with everything they had of energy and enthusiasm.

U.S. President Harry S. Truman

Dullness is the one sin there is no absolution for.

Jack Valenti, movie executive

Enthusiasm is that secret and harmonious spirit which hovers over the production of genius

Isaac Disraeli, British writer and scholar

Success is going from one failure to failure without losing your enthusiasm.

Sir Winston Churchill, British Prime Minister

Before you can inspire with emotion, you must be swamped with it yourself. Before you can move their tears, your own must flow. To convince them, you must yourself believe.

Sir Winston Churchill, British Prime Minister

You got to lively up yourself and don't be no drag. You got to lively up yourself cause it really isn't all that bad.

Bob Marley, live at the Lyceum Theatre

When a man dies, if he can pass enthusiasm along to his children, he has left them an estate of incalculable value.

Thomas A. Edison, inventor

A mediocre idea that generates enthusiasm will go further than a great idea that inspires no one.

Mary Kay Ash, founder of *Mary Kay Cosmetics*

The worst bankruptcy in the world is the person who has lost his enthusiasm.

H. W. Arnold, author

In things pertaining to enthusiasm, no man is sane who does not know how to be insane on proper occasions.

Henry Ward Beecher, clergyman and abolitionist

A man can succeed at almost anything for which he has unlimited enthusiasm.

Charles M. Schwab, American steel magnate

I consider my ability to arouse enthusiasm among people the greatest asset I possess and the way to develop the best that is in a person is by appreciation and encouragement. There is nothing else that kills the ambitions of a person as criticisms from superiors. I never criticize anyone. I believe in giving a person an incentive to work. So I'm anxious to praise but loath to find fault. If I like anything I'm hearty in my approval and lavish in my praise.

Charles M. Schwab, American steel magnate

I am seeking. I am striving. I am in it with all my heart.

Vincent Van Gogh, painter

The greatest intellectual capacities are only found in a vehement and passionate will.

Arthur Schopenhauer, philosopher

If you have the will to win, you have achieved half your success; if you don't, you have achieved half your failure.

David Ambrose, writer

Zeal is a volcano, the peak of which the grass of indecisiveness does not grow.

Kahlil Gibran, artist and philosopher

No pessimist ever discovered the secret of the stars, or sailed to an uncharted land or opened a new doorway for the human spirit.

Helen Keller, author and activist

I feel sorry for the person who can't get genuinely excited about his work. Not only will he never be satisfied, but he will never achieve anything worthwhile.

Walter Chrysler, automotive entrepreneur

The real secret of success is enthusiasm.

Walter Chrysler, automotive entrepreneur

Every person's feelings have a front-door and a side-door by which they may be entered.

Oliver Wendell Holmes, Jr., U.S. Supreme Court Justice

He that rides his hobby gently must always give way to him that rides his hobby hard.

An old English proverb

I prefer the folly of enthusiasm to the indifference of wisdom

Anatole France, French poet

Let us endeavor to live so that when we come to die, even the undertaker will be sorry.

Mark Twain, writer

Nobody really cares if you're miserable, so you might as well be happy.

Cynthia Nelms, writer

You're only given a little spark of madness. You mustn't lose it.

Robin Williams, comedian and actor

Enthusiasm: the sustaining power of all great action.

Samuel Smiles, Scottish author and reformer

Enthusiasm is the electricity of life. How do you get it? You act enthusiastic until you make it a habit.

Gordon Parks, artist and novelist

A great drive, a powerful determination and a consuming desire will easily compensate for little or limited talent.
> Dr. Robert Schuller, spiritual leader

Only passions, great passions, can elevate the soul to great things.
> Denis Diderot, philosopher

Energy flows where attention goes
> Stuart Wilde, metaphysical author

Life's blows cannot break a person whose spirit is warmed at the fire of enthusiasm.
> Dr. Norman Vincent Peale, spiritual leader

If you are not getting as much from life as you want to, then examine the state of your enthusiasm.
> Dr. Norman Vincent Peale, spiritual leader

Enthusiasm releases the drive to carry you over obstacles and adds significance to all you do
> Dr. Norman Vincent Peale, spiritual leader

If you have zest and enthusiasm you attract zest and enthusiasm. Life does give back in kind.
> Dr. Norman Vincent Peale, spiritual leader

Throw your heart over the fence and the rest will follow.
> Dr. Norman Vincent Peale, spiritual leader

A salesman minus enthusiasm is just a clerk.
> Harry F. Banks, author

Wherever you go, go with all your heart.
> Confucius, Chinese philosopher

Chapter 9

Smile, Laugh and Have a Pleasing Personality

A man without a smiling face must not open a shop.
Chinese proverb

Laughter is the shortest distance between two people.
Victor Borge, comedian

You can accomplish by kindness what you cannot by force.
Publilius Syrus, Roman philosopher

The happy man is not he who seems thus to others, but who seems thus to himself.
Publilius Syrus, Roman philosopher

Smile well and often. It makes people wonder what you're up to.
Satchel Paige, baseball player

There can never be enough said of the virtues, dangers, and the power of a shared laugh.
Francoise Sagan, French playwright

Of all the things you wear, your expression is the most important.
Janet Lane

Lighten up Francis.
From the movie *Stripes*

Unextinguished laughter shakes the sky.
Homer, from the *Iliad*

Beauty is power; a smile is its sword.
Charles Reade, English novelist

No one is laughable who laughs at himself.
Seneca, Roman philosopher

If someone is too tired to give you a smile, leave one of your own, because no one needs a smile as much as those who have none to give.
Samson Hirsch, educator

The most wasted day is that in which we have not laughed.
Nicolas Chamfort, French writer

Laughter is an instant vacation.
Milton Berle, comedian

It takes 26 muscles to smile, and 62 muscles to frown.
Author unknown

When people are laughing, they're generally not killing each other.
Alan Alda, actor

He who laughs best today, will also laugh last.
Friedrich Nietzsche, German philosopher

A smile is the universal welcome.
Max Eastman, writer

What soap is to the body, laughter is to the soul.
Jewish proverb

I am a reverse paranoid, I think everyone's out to make me happy.
Author unknown

I've always thought that a big laugh is a really loud noise from the soul saying, "Ain't that the truth!"
Quincy Jones, music entrepreneur

Against the assault of laughter nothing can stand.
Mark Twain, American author

Wrinkles should merely indicate where smiles have been.
Mark Twain, American author

Smile, it increases your face value.
Cosmetics advertisement

A smile cures the wounding of a frown.
William Shakespeare, English poet and playwright

The best of healers is good cheer.
Pindar, Greek poet

Mirth is God's medicine. Everybody ought to bathe in it.
Henry Ward Beecher, clergyman and abolitionist

People seldom notice old clothes if you wear a big smile.
Lee Mildon

A warm smile is the universal language of kindness.
William A. Ward, American writer

If we couldn't laugh we would all go insane.
Jimmy Buffet, musician

Most smiles are started by another smile.
Author unknown

A smile is a curve that sets everything straight.
Phyllis Diller, actress and comedian

Before you put on a frown, make absolutely sure there are no smiles available.
Jim Beggs, writer

A laugh is a smile that bursts.
Mary Waldrip, author

A man isn't poor if he can still laugh.
Raymond Hitchcock, actor and writer

Be kind, for everyone you meet is fighting a harder battle.

Plato, Greek philosopher

Let no one ever come to you without leaving better and happier.

Mother Teresa, Roman Catholic missionary

Peace begins with a smile.

Mother Teresa, Roman Catholic missionary

When I was walking down the street, I just smile and let them all think, "That guy's having a good day!"

W. Phillip Walsh, financial advisor

He that is of a merry heart hath a continual feast.

Proverbs 15:15

Whoever is happy will make others happy too.

Anne Frank, Holocaust diarist

At the height of laughter, the universe is flung into a kaleidoscope of new possibilities.

Jean Houston, PhD., author and philosopher

Carry laughter with you wherever you go.

Hugh Sidey, journalist

A cloudy day is no match for a sunny disposition.

William Arthur Ward, American writer

If you lose the power to laugh, you lose the power to think.

Clarence Darrow, lawyer

Remember, men need laughter sometimes more than food.

Anna Fellows Johnston, author

Dad always said laughter was the best medicine, which I guess is why several of us died of tuberculosis.

From *Deep Thoughts by Jack Handey*

Laughter gives us distance. It allows us to step back from an event, deal with it and then move on.

Bob Newhart, comedian and actor

A good laugh and a long sleep are the best cures in the doctor's book.

An old Irish saying

Laughter is the sun that drives winter from the face.

Victor Hugo, French poet

The friendly smile, the word of greeting, are certainly something fleeting and seemingly insubstantial. You can't take them with you. But they work for good beyond your power to measure their influence.

J C Penney, retailer

If you want to be happy, be.

Leo Tolstoy, Russian author

Everyone smiles in the same language

Author unknown

Never frown because you never know who might be falling in love with your smile.

Justine Milton, journalist

Chapter 10

Ask for the Order . . .
Again and Again and Again!

You've got to ask! Asking is, in my opinion, the world's most powerful and neglected secret to success and happiness.

Percy Ross, columnist and philanthropist

Timid salespeople have skinny children.

Zig Ziglar, sales and motivational author

Ask, and it shall be given you; seek; and you shall find; knock and it shall be opened unto you. For every one that asketh receiveth; and he that seeketh findeth; and to him that knocketh it shall be opened.

Matthew 7:7-8

I attribute my success to two things: One, I know what I want. Two, I am not afraid to ask for it in a direct way. I am always direct about what I want and I always get it.

Sharon Stone, actress

If you don't ask—you don't get.

Mahatma Gandhi, spiritual and political leader of India

You can't ask for what you want unless you know what it is. A lot of people don't know what they want or they want much less than they deserve. First you have figure out what you want. Second, you have to decide that you deserve it. Third, you have to believe you can get it. And, fourth, you have to have the guts to ask for it.

Dr. Barbara De Angelis, relationship expert

Asking is the beginning of receiving. Make sure you don't go to the ocean with a teaspoon. At least take a bucket so the kids won't laugh at you.

Jim Rohn, motivational writer

There are too fools in every market: One asks too little, one asks too much.

> Russian proverb

Chance is always powerful. Let your hook be always cast; in the stream where you least expect it, there will be a fish.

> Ovid, Roman poet

Ask with urgency and passion.

> Arthur James Balfour, British Prime Minister

Man who waits for roast duck to fly into mouth must wait very, very long time.

> Chinese proverb

Even the gods are moved by the voice of entreaty.

> J. Lewis May, author

Great things are only possible with outrageous requests.

> Thea Alexander, psychologist and author

Not to ask is not to be denied.

> John Dryden, English poet

The time to stop talking is when the other person nods his head affirmatively, but says nothing.

> Author unknown

He who asks is a fool for five minutes, but he who does not ask remains a fool forever.

> Chinese proverb

You don't always get what you ask for, but you never get what you don't ask for . . . unless it's contagious.

> Beverly Sills, Opera Singer

Learn to ask for what you want. The worst people can do is not give you what you ask for—which is precisely where you were before you asked.

> Peter McWilliams, author

If you are not moving closer to what you want in sales, you probably aren't doing enough asking.

Jack Canfield, writer and success coach

People who ask confidently get more than those who are hesitant and uncertain. When you've figured out what you want to ask for, do it with certainty, boldness and confidence.

Jack Canfield, writer and success coach

Some people fold after making one timid request. They quit too soon. Keep asking until you find the answers. In sales there are usually four or five "no's" before you get a "yes."

Jack Canfield, writer and success coach

A clever, imagination, humorous request can open closed doors and closed minds.

Percy Ross, columnist and philanthropist

The world is full of genies waiting to grant your wishes.

Percy Ross, columnist and philanthropist

Better to ask twice than to lose your way once.

Danish Proverb

If there is something to gain and nothing to lose by asking, by all means, ask!

W. Clement Stone, insurance executive and motivational author

You create your opportunities by asking for them.

Shakti Gwain, spiritual author

The righteous cry and the Lord heareth, and delivereth them out of all their troubles.

Psalm 37:17

You'll always miss 100% of the shots you don't take.

Wayne Gretzky, hockey player

Ask with urgency and passion.

Arthur James Balfour, British politician

If there is something to gain and nothing to lose by asking, by all means ask!

W. Clement Stone, insurance executive

Close early and close often!

Old sales adage

Chapter 11

Overcoming Objections and Rejection

I am dyslexic; the word "NO" turns me on!
Carl Mather, executive recruiter

When pessimists confront you, know your product and use the facts.
William O'Neil, publisher of Investor's Business Daily

A boy carries out suggestions more wholeheartedly when he understands their aim.
Sir Robert Baden-Powell, founder of the *Boy Scouts*

I take rejection as someone blowing a bugle in my ear to wake up and get going, rather than retreat.
Sylvester Stallone, actor and writer

He who knows only his own side of the case knows little of that.
John Stuart Mill, British philosopher and statesman

Despite the rejection and in violation of all the rules, I came back year after year.
Joseph Barbera, cartoon genius

Don't go into the barn without a shovel.
H. Ross Perot, billionaire

Some actors couldn't figure out how to withstand the constant rejection. They couldn't see the light at the end of the tunnel.
Harrison Ford, actor

Through my illness I learned rejection. I was written off. That was the moment I thought, okay, game on. No prisoners. Everybody's going down.
Lance Armstrong, seven time winner of the *Tour de France*

Agreement is made more precious by disagreement
Publilius Syrus, Roman philosopher

You have to love this business. You have to be able to take rejection.
Jessica Biel, actress

It's the constant and determined effort that breaks down the resistance, sweeps away all obstacles.
Claude M. Bristol, journalist and motivational author

An objection is not rejection; it is simply a request for more information.
Bo Bennett, entrepreneur and author

A rejection is nothing more than a necessary step in the pursuit of success.
Bo Bennett, entrepreneur and author

Every rejection is incremental payment on dues that in some way will be translated back into your work.
James Lee Burke, author

Fall down seven times, get up eight.
An old Indian saying

Over emphatic negatives always suggest that what is being denied may be what is really being asserted.
Jonathan Raban, British author

A hungry stomach has no ears.
La Fontaine, French poet

Men are not against you; they are merely for themselves.
Gene Fowler, journalist

Look up the definition of rejection in the dictionary; get really comfortable with it, and then maybe you can go into acting.
Loni Anderson, actress

The human mind treats a new idea the way the body treats a strange protein; it rejects it.
Sir Peter Medawar, British scientist

He who knows the road can ride at full trot.
Italian proverb

Practice, practice, practice until you eventually get numb on rejections.
Brian Klemmer, author

If you know the enemy and know yourself, you need not fear the results of a hundred battles.
Sun Tzu, author of *The Art of War*

I was told to avoid the business all together because of the rejection. People would say to me, 'Don't you want to have a normal job and a normal family?' I guess that would be good advice for some people, but I wanted to act.
Jennifer Aniston, actress

The writer of M.A.S.H. was rejected by 32 producers because the idea was too off-the-wall. Sylvester Stallone was rejected by over 1,000 agents while he was pitching his own acting career and writing Rocky. Ted Geisel's (Dr. Seuss) first book was rejected by 86 publishers. The Wizard of OZ was rejected by over 50 different producers and one said, "I see no value here." The secret to success in any business is massive rejection!
Author unknown

You may have to fight a battle more than once to win it.
Margaret Thatcher, British Prime Minister

Stand up to your obstacles and do something about them. You will find that they haven't half the strength you think they have.
Dr. Norman Vincent Peale, spiritual leader

Fighting fire with fire only gets you ashes!
Abigail van Buren, advice columnist

Keep cool; anger is not an argument.

Daniel Webster, statesman

Three quarters of the miseries and misunderstanding in the world would finish if people were to put on the shoes of their adversaries and understood their points of view.

Mahatma Gandhi, spiritual and political leader of India

Seek first to understand, then to be understood.

Stephen Covey, author and management consultant

We keep going back, stronger, not weaker, because we will not allow rejection to beat us down. It will only strengthen our resolve. To be successful there is no other way.

Earl G. Graves, entrepreneur and publisher

Patience and perseverance have a magical effect before which difficulties disappear and obstacles vanish."

U.S. President John Quincy Adams

Chapter 12

Be Yourself and Use Your Personal Assets

Too many people overvalue what they are not, and undervalue what they are.

> Malcolm Forbes, magazine publisher

I think knowing what you cannot do is more important than knowing what you can do.

> Lucille Ball, actress

The most important part of the salesperson is the person.

> Zig Ziglar, sales trainer and author

My mother said to me, "If you become a soldier, you'll be a general; if you become a monk you'll end up as the pope." Instead, I became a painter and wound up as Picasso.

> Pablo Picasso, artist

Just be yourself Sir—whatever happens, they can't take that away from you.

> Coleman the butler, from the movie *Trading Places*

Do what you can with what you have, where you are.

> U.S. President Theodore Roosevelt

Don't be sharp or flat; just be natural.

> Willie Stargell, baseball player

Be what you are. This is the first step toward becoming better than you are.

> J.C. Hare

The crow that mimics the cormorant gets drowned.

Japanese proverb

What we must decide is how we are valuable, rather than how valuable we are.

F. Scott Fitzgerald, author

It is a great mistake to think you are more than you are and yet to underestimate your real value.

Johann Wolfgang Von Goethe, German writer

No man was ever a great by imitation.

Samuel Johnson, English writer

To be nobody but yourself—in a world that is doing its best, night and day, to make you everybody else—means to fight the hardest battle that any human being can fight, and never stop fighting.

E.E Cummings, poet

Since God made us to be originals, why stoop to be a copy?

Reverend Billy Graham, spiritual leader

Be who you are and say what you feel because those who mind don't matter and those who matter don't mind.

Ted Geisel (Dr. Seuss), author

Use what talent you possess: the woods would be very silent if no birds sang except those that sang best.

Henry Van Dyke, educator and diplomat

Hide not your talents. They for use were made. What's a sundial in the shade?

Benjamin Franklin, statesman

Everybody must row with the oars he has.

Old English saying

Whenever you do something new, whenever you do something unusual, whenever you do something contrary to the accepted wisdom, you have to be the first to do it. The second one may succeed, the third one may succeed, but there is a major advantage to being first.
Andrew A. Lanyi, Holocaust Survivor and stockbroker

Trust the instinct to the end, though you can render no reason.
Ralph Waldo Emerson, philosopher

Make yourself necessary to someone.
Ralph Waldo Emerson, philosopher

Instinct is the sum total of all your life experiences.
Chris Maloney

Be a good animal, true to your animal instinct.
D.H. Lawrence, English writer

I complained that I had no shoes until I met a man who had no feet.
Author unknown

He who blames his tools is a poor carpenter.
Confucius, Chinese philosopher

Historically, good men with poor ships have fared better than poor men with good ships.
U.S. Admiral J.K. Taussig

All great things begin as blasphemies.
George Bernard Shaw, Irish playwright

Only dead fish swim with the current.
Templeton Mutual Fund advertisement

The grass is always greener on the greener side.
Michelle Shocked, singer and songwriter

If a man does not keep pace with his companions, perhaps it is because he hears a different drummer. Let him step to the music which he hears, however measured or far away.

Henry David Thoreau, writer and philosopher

Trust yourself. You know more than you think you do.

Benjamin Spock, M.D.

Ignorant men don't know what good they hold in their hands until they've flung it away.

Sophocles, Greek playwright

There is always some beauty left, in nature, sunshine, freedom, in yourself. These can all help you. Look at these things, then you find yourself again and God. And then you regain your balance.

Anne Frank, Holocaust diarist

The hardest arithmetic to master is that which enables us to count our blessings.

Eric Hoffer, philosopher

He is a wise man who does not grieve for the things he has not, but rejoices for those which he has.

Epictetus, Greek philosopher

If we did the things we were capable of doing, we would literally astound ourselves.

Thomas Edison, inventor

We are haunted by an ideal life and it is because we have within us the beginning and the possibility of it.

Phillips Brooks, clergyman

Your imperfections are what make you beautiful.

Sandra Bullock, actress

Compared to what we ought to be, we are only half awake. We are making use of only a small part of our physical and mental resources. Stating the thin broadly, the human individual thus lives far within his limits. He possesses powers of various sorts which he habitually fails to use.

> William James, psychologist and philosopher

If the doors of perception were cleansed, everything would appear to man as it is, infinite.

> William Blake, English poet

I feel strongly that the visual arts are of vast importance. Of course, I could be prejudiced. I am a visual art!

> Kermit the frog, Muppet

Silly is you in a natural state, and serious is something you have to do until you can get silly again.

> Mike Myers, actor

Life is too important to be taken seriously.

> Oscar Wilde, Irish author

Yesterday is a cancelled check. Tomorrow is a promissory note. Today is the only cash you have, so spend it wisely.

> Kim Lyons, athlete and fitness model

Anything you're good at contributes to happiness.

> Bertrand Russell, mathematician and philosopher

He that is neither one thing nor the other has no friends.

> Aesop, Greek philosopher

Anybody who is any good is different from anybody else.

Felix Frankfuter, U.S. Supreme Court Justice

This above all: To thine own self be true, and it must follow, as the night and the day, thou canst not be false to any man.

William Shakespeare, English poet and playwright

Do what you can, with what you have, where you are.

U.S. President Theodore Roosevelt

Whoever you are, there is some younger person who thinks you are perfect. There is some work that will never be done if you don't do it. There is someone who would miss you if you were gone. There is a place that you alone can fill.

Jacob Braude, author

We are all born originals. Why is it so many of us die copies?

Edward Young, poet and author

Chapter 13

Self Promotion, Advertising and Public Relations

If you think advertising doesn't work, consider the millions of Americans that now think yogurt tastes good.
> Joe L. Whitley

Many a small thing has been made large by the right kind of advertising.
> Mark Twain, American author

A rooster crows only when it sees the light. Put him in the dark and he'll never crow. I have seen the light and I'm crowing.
> Muhammad Ali, boxer

I am the greatest; I said that even before I knew I was.
> Muhammad Ali, boxer

I figured that if I said it enough, I would convince the world that I really was the greatest.
> Muhammad Ali, boxer

It's hard to be humble, when you're as great as I am.
> Muhammad Ali, boxer

It's not bragging if you can back it up.
> Muhammad Ali, boxer

Advertising is like learning—a little can be dangerous.
> P.T. Barnum, circus operator and showman

Early to bed, early to rise, work like hell, and advertise.
> Laurence J. Peter, advertising executive

Advertising is the "wonder" in Wonder Bread.

Jeff Richards, advertising consultant

In general, my children refused to eat anything that hadn't danced on TV.

Erma Bombeck, humorist and author

Advertising nourishes the consuming power of men. It sets up before a man the goal of a better home, better clothing, better food for himself and his family. It spurs individual exertion and greater production.

Sir Winston Churchill, British Prime Minister

Promise, large promise, is the soul of an advertisement.

Samuel Johnson, English author

Society drives people crazy with lust and calls it advertising

John Lahr, theater critic

If you don't find it in the index, look very carefully through the entire catalogue.

Sears Catalog

The secret of all effective originality in advertising is not the creation of new and tricky words and pictures, but one of putting familiar words and pictures into new relationships.

Leo Burnett, advertising executive

The Greatest Sales Strategy in the world: Don't tell me how good you make it; tell me how it makes me when I use it.

Leo Burnett, advertising executive

Advertising says to people, 'Here's what we've got. Here's what it will do for you. Here's how to get it.

Leo Burnett, advertising executive

Good advertising does not just circulate information. It penetrates the public mind with desires and belief.

Leo Burnett, advertising executive

Make it simple. Make it memorable. Make it inviting to look at. Make it fun to read.

Leo Burnett, advertising executive

Plan the sale when you plan the ad.

Leo Burnett, advertising executive

Advertising is the ability to sense, interpret . . . to put the very heart throbs of a business into type, paper and ink.

Leo Burnett, advertising executive

In marketing I've seen only one strategy that can't miss and that is to market to your best customers first, your best prospects second and the rest of the world last.

John Romero

The more facts you tell, the more you sell. An advertisement's chance for success invariably increases as the number of pertinent merchandise facts included in the ad increases.

Dr Charles Edwards

If you make a product good enough even though you live in the depths of the forest, the public will make a path to your door, says the philosopher. But if you want the public in sufficient numbers, you had better construct a highway. Advertise is that highway.

William Randolph Hearst, publisher

Give them quality. That's the best kind of advertising.

Milton Hershey, candy manufacturer

You, me, all of us must turn ourselves into distinctive one-person brands.

Tom Peters, business author

It ain't bragging if you really done it.

Dizzy Dean, baseball player

We find that advertising works the way the grass grows. You can never see it, but every week you have to mow the lawn.

Andy Tarshis, businessman

Yes, I sell people things they don't need. I can't, however, sell them something they don't want. Even with advertising—even if I were of a mind to.

> John O'Toole

To establish oneself in the world, one does all one can to seem established there already.

> La Rochefoucauld, French author

I believe in capitalism as the best way to improve the lives of most of the people of South Africa, and advertising is the petrol that fuels a capitalist system.

> Ross Chowles, advertising executive

It has become a certainty now that if you will only advertise sufficiently you may make a fortune by selling anything.

> Anthony Trollope, English novelist

Things do not pass for what they are, but for what they seem. Most things are judged by their jackets.

> Baltasar Gracian, Spanish writer

The philosophy behind much advertising is based on the old observation that every man is really two men; the man he is and the man he wants to be.

> William Feather, publisher and author

The final key to the way I promote is bravado. I play to people's fantasies. People may not always think big themselves, but they can still get very excited by those who do. That's why a little hyperbole never hurts.

> Donald Trump, real estate magnate

If you done it, it ain't bragging.

> Walt Whitman, American writer

Doing business without advertising is like winking at a girl in the dark. You know what you are doing, but nobody else does."

> Steuart Henderson Britt, advertising executive and author

In good times, people want to advertise; in bad times, they have to.

Bruce Barton, advertising executive

Advertising is of the very essence of democracy. An election goes on every minute of the business day across the counters of hundreds of thousands of stores and shops where the customers state their preferences and determine which manufacturer and which product shall be the leader today, and which shall lead tomorrow.

Bruce Barton, advertising executive

Advertising is salesmanship mass produced. No one would bother to use advertising if he could talk to all his prospects face-to-face. But he can't.

Morris Hite, advertising executive

There is more money wasted in advertising by underspending than by overspending. Years ago someone said that underspending in advertising is like buying a ticket halfway to Europe. You've spent your money but you never get there.

Morris Hite, advertising executive

So long as there's a jingle in your head, television isn't free.

Jason Love, cartoonist

The only way to advertise is by not focusing on the product.

Calvin Klein, fashion designer

Great ideas need landing gear as well as wings.

C.D. Jackson, publisher of Life Magazine

The business that considers itself immune to the necessity for advertising sooner or later finds itself immune to business.

Derby Brown, businessman

It has taken more than a hundred scientists two years to find out how to make the product in question; I have been given thirty days to create its personality and plan its launching. If I do my job well, I shall contribute as much as the hundred scientists to the success of this product.

David Ogilvy, advertising executive

The best ideas come as jokes. Make your thinking as funny as possible.
David Ogilvy, advertising executive

Don't bunt. Aim out of the ball park. Aim for the company of immortals.
David Ogilvy, advertising executive

I do not regard advertising as entertainment or an art form, but as a medium of information.
David Ogilvy, advertising executive

I don't know the rules of grammar. If you're trying to persuade people to do something, or buy something, it seems to me you should use their language.
David Ogilvy, advertising executive

Advertising may be described as the science of arresting the human intelligence long enough to get money from it.
Stephen Butler Leacock, writer and economist

Chapter 14

Dress and Personal Appearance

Clothes can suggest, persuade, connote, insinuate, or indeed lie, and apply subtle pressure while their wearer is speaking frankly and straightforwardly of other matters.

Anne Hollander, fashion writer

Dress for Success.

John T. Molloy, author

Even I don't wake up looking like Cindy Crawford.

Cindy Crawford, supermodel

A man becomes the creature of his uniform.

Napoleon Bonaparte, French military and political leader

Appearance rules the world.

Johann Friedrich Von Schiller, German philosopher and poet

They come running just as fast as they can because every girl's crazy about a sharp dressed man.

Sharp Dressed Man, by ZZ Top

When I call on a client, I come by cab and I am sleek and clean and foursquare. I carry myself as though I made a quiet killing in the stock market and have come to call more as a public service than anything else.

Kurt Vonnegut, writer

Regardless of how you feel inside, always try to look like a winner.

Arthur Ashe, tennis player

Cleanliness is indeed next to Godliness.

John Wesley, theologian

Clothes are inevitable. They are nothing less than the furniture of the mind made visible.

James Laver, costume historian

Clothes are never a frivolity; they always mean something.

James Laver, costume historian

Good clothes open all doors.

Thomas Fuller, M.D.

A good presence is letters of recommendation.

Thomas Fuller, M.D.

A man, in order to establish himself in the world, does everything he can to appear established there.

La Rochefoucauld, French writer

Keep thy shop and thy shop will keep thee.

British proverb

Clothes and manners do not make the man, but when he is made, they greatly improve his appearances.

Henry Ward Beecher, clergyman and abolitionist

The apparel oft proclaims the man.

William Shakespeare, English poet and playwright

Costly thy habit as thy purse can buy, but not expressed in fancy; rich not gaudy; for the apparel oft proclaims the man.

William Shakespeare, English poet and playwright

I have heard with admiring submission the experience of the lady who declared that the sense of being perfectly well-dressed gives a feeling of inward tranquility which religion is powerless to bestow.

Ralph Waldo Emerson, philosopher

People laughed at the way I dressed, but that was the secret of my success. I didn't look like anyone.

Coco Chanel, fashion designer

Fashion is architecture; it is a matter of proportions.
Coco Chanel, fashion designer

Adornment is never anything except a reflection of the heart.
Coco Chanel, clothes designer

Fashion is more powerful than the tyrant.
Latin saying

I love America, and I love American women. But there is one thing that deeply shocks me—American closets. I cannot believe one can dress well when you have so much.
Andree Putman, French designer

A man with a good coat upon his back meets with a better reception than he who has a bad one.
Samuel Johnson, English writer

Every hair makes its shadow on the ground.
Spanish proverb

Know, first, who you are; and then adorn yourself accordingly.
Epictetus, Greek philosopher

You'd be surprised how much it costs to look this cheap.
Dolly Parton, country music star

When in doubt, wear red.
Bill Blass, designer

Clothes make the man. Naked people have little or no influence on society.
Mark Twain, American author

What a strange power there is in clothing.
Isaac Bashevis, Singer

Every time a woman leaves off something she looks better, but every time a man leaves off something, he looks worse.
Will Rogers, humorist and comedian

Almost every man looks more so in a belted trench coat.

Sydney J. Harris, journalist

Fashion can be bought. Style one must possess.

Edna Woolman Chase, editor of *Vogue*

One should either be a work of art, or wear a work of art.

Oscar Wilde, Irish author

Like every good man, I strive for perfection, and like every ordinary man, I have found that perfection is out of reach—but not the perfect suit.

Edward Tivnan, writer

The dress must not hang on the body but follow its lines. It must accompany its wearer and when a woman smiles the dress must smile with her.

Madeleine Vionnet, French fashion designer

I have often said that I wish I had invented blue jeans: the most spectacular, the most practical, the most relaxed and nonchalant. They have expression, modesty, sex appeal, simplicity—all I hope for in my clothes.

Yves Saint Laurent, clothes designer

Carelessness in dressing is moral suicide.

Balzac, French novelist and playwright

Your business clothes are naturally attracted to staining liquids. This attraction is strongest just before an important meeting.

Scott Adams, creator of the Dilbert Comic strip

If honor be your clothing, the suit will last a lifetime; but if clothing be your honor, it will soon be worn threadbare.

William Arnot, Scottish minister

Seldom do people discern eloquence under a threadbare cloak.

Juvenal, Roman poet

Never wear anything that panics the cat.

P.J. O'Rourke, writer

Cleanliness becomes important when godliness is unlikely.
P.J. O'Rourke, writer

I hold that gentleman to be the best dressed whose dress no one observes.
Anthony Trollope, writer

When in doubt, wear red.
Bill Blass, fashion designer

There is much to support the view that it is clothes that wear us and not we them; we may make them take the mould of arm or breast, but they would mould our hearts, our brains, our tongues to their liking.
Virginia Wolf, English novelist

What a strange power there is in clothing.
Isaac Bashevis Singer, Nobel Prize winner and Yiddish writer

Funny that a pair of really nice shoes make us feel good in our heads, at the extreme opposite end of our bodies.
Levende Waters

It is an interesting question how far men would retain their relative rank if they were divested of their clothes.
Henry David Thoreau, writer and philosopher

You're never fully dressed without a smile.
From the play *Annie*

Step Four

Know Your Goals, Have a Plan and Take Action

Think Big

Goal Setting: Dream it, See it, Say it and Believe it!

Planning and Preparation

Discipline, Daily Focus and Good Habits

Time Management

Sales Leaders are Team Builders

Decide and Take Action Now!

Take Risks and Make Mistakes

Chapter 15

Think Big!

If you aren't going all the way, why go at all?
Joe Namath, football player

It's never too late to be what you might have been.
George Eliot, English novelist

Make no small plans for they have not the power to stir men's blood.
Niccolo Machiavelli, Italian diplomat and philosopher

It is a funny thing about life; if you refuse to accept anything but the best, you very often get it.
W. Somerset Maugham, English playwright

If you're going to think, you might as well think BIG. Thinking small and thinking big takes the same amount of energy.
Donald Trump, real estate magnate

As long as you're going to be thinking anyway, think big.
Donald Trump, real estate magnate

I wasn't satisfied just to earn a good living. I was looking to make a statement.
Donald Trump, real estate magnate

The best way to help the poor is to not be one of them.
Donald Trump, real estate magnate

Knowledge is limited. Imagination encircles the world.
Albert Einstein, scientist

Babe Ruth was asked in a press interview after his career was over what his greatest failure in life was? The Babe replied, "Hitting a home run with no one on base."

Author unknown

If we did all the things we were capable of doing, we would literally astonish ourselves.

Thomas A. Edison, inventor

Charlie, don't forget about the man who got everything he wanted . . . he lived happily ever after.

From the movie, *Willy Wonka and the Chocolate Factory*

You must be the change you wish to see in the world.

Mahatma Gandhi, political and spiritual leader of India

We are what we think. All that we are arises with our thoughts. With our thoughts, we make the world.

Buddha, founder of Buddhism

Shoot for the moon. Even if you miss, you will land amongst the stars.

Author unknown

One can never consent to creep when one feels an impulse to soar.

Helen Keller, author and activist

Man is what he believes.

Anton Chekhov, writer

Our life is what our thoughts make it.

Marcus Aurelis, Roman Emperor

I think, therefore I am.

Descartes, French philosopher

The direction of the mind is more important than its progress.

Joseph Joubert, French essayist

The mind is its own place and in itself can make a heaven of hell, a hell of heaven.
From *Paradise Lost*

Don't bunt. Aim out of the ballpark. Aim for the company of immortals.
David Ogilvy, advertising executive

Price high, then justify.
From, The *Four Hour Work Week*

Don't be afraid to give up the good to go for the great.
John D. Rockefeller, oil titan

Create the highest, grandest vision possible for your life, because you become what you believe.
Oprah Winfrey, media mogul and billionaire

I always knew I was destined for greatness
Oprah Winfrey, media mogul and billionaire

I don't think of myself as a poor deprived ghetto girl who made good. I think of myself as somebody who from an early age knew I was responsible for myself, and I had to make good.
Oprah Winfrey, media mogul and billionaire

When I look into the future, it's so bright it burns my eyes.
Oprah Winfrey, media mogul and billionaire

Do not follow the ideas of others, but learn to listen to the voice within yourself. Your body and mind will become clear and you will realize the unity of all things.
Dogen, Buddhist philosopher

I want to put a ding in the universe.
Steve Jobs, founder of Apple

Do not go where the path may lead, go instead where there is no path and leave a
Ralph Waldo Emerson, philosopher

In the long run, men hit only what they aim at. Therefore, they had better aim at something high.

Henry David Thoreau, writer and philosopher

I'm not the greatest; I'm the double greatest. Not only do I knock 'em out, I pick the round.

Muhammad Ali, boxer

Superman don't need no seat belt.

Muhammad Ali, boxer

Fake it until you make it!

Old motivational saying

Chapter 16

Goal Setting: Dream it, See it,
Say it and Believe it!

Reality is wrong. Dreams are for real.

> Tupak Shakur, musician

What the mind can conceive and believe it can achieve.

> Napoleon Hill, from *Think and Grow Rich*

A goal is a dream with a deadline.

> Napoleon Hill, from *Think and Grow Rich*

More gold has been mined from the thoughts of men than has been taken from the earth.

> Napoleon Hill, from *Think and Grow Rich*

It's the repetition of affirmations that leads to belief. And once that belief becomes a deep conviction, things begin to happen.

> Muhammad Ali, boxer

You'll see it when you believe it.

> Dr. Wayne W. Dyer, spiritual writer

The first step to becoming is to will it.

> Mother Teresa, Roman Catholic missionary

I dream my painting and then I paint my dream.

> Vincent Van Gogh, painter

It doesn't matter where you are coming from. All that matters is where you are going.

> Brian Tracy, sales trainer

Don't let other people tell you what you want.
>Pat Riley, basketball coach

Everything you now have is the result of a goal.
>Anthony Robbins, success trainer and author

Obstacles cannot crush me. Every obstacle yields to stern resolve. He who is fixed to a star does not change his mind.
>Leonardo Da Vinci, inventor

Each moment of our life, we either invoke or destroy our dreams. We call upon it to become a fact or we cancel our previous instructions.
>Stuart Wilde, metaphysical author

The thing always happens that you really believe in; and the belief in a thing makes it happen.
>Frank Lloyd Wright, architect

The world makes way for the man who knows where he is going.
>Ralph Waldo Emerson, philosopher

Do not follow the ideas of others, but learn to listen to the voice within yourself. Your body and mind will become clear and you will become clear and you will realize the unity of all things.
>Dogen, Buddhist monk

With a goal in life you have to be like a postage stamp: it sticks to one thing until it gets there.
>Josh Billings, writer and humorist

Talent hits a target no one else can hit; Genius hits a target no one else can see.
>Arthur Schopenhauer, German philosopher

God gave me everything I want.
>Mick Jagger, the Rolling Stones

We choose our joys and sorrows long before we experience them.
>Kahlil Gibran, Lebanese artist and poet

You have to be very careful; if you don't know where you are going, you might not get there.

Yogi Berra, baseball player

Your imagination is your preview of life's coming attractions.

Albert Einstein, scientist

If you want to live a happy life, tie it to a goal, not to people or things.

Albert Einstein, scientist

Great minds have purposes, others have dreams.

Washington Irving, author

The most important thing about having goals is having one.

Geoffrey Abert, French philosopher

Give me a stock clerk with a goal and I will give you a man who will make history. Give me a man without a goal and I will give you a stock clerk.

J.C. Penny, retailer

Long range goals keep you from being frustrated by short term failures.

J.C. Penny, retailer

Looking back may be tempting, but it's terribly counterproductive. Pour your energy, every bit of it, into adapting to your new world.

Andrew Grove, technology executive

Man is not the sum of what he has already, but the sum of what he does not yet have, of what he could have.

Jean-Paul Sartre, French philosopher and playwright

The indispensable first step to getting the things you want out of life is this: decide what you want!

Ben Stein, writer and actor

If you don't know where you're going, any road will take you there.

George Harrison, musician

At the age of 24, I began setting clear written goals for each area of my life. I accomplished more in the following year than I did in the previous 24.

Brian Tracy, sales trainer

It's not just the emotional, intellectual, and physical gaps between you and money. The real gap is always between what you think you want and what you actually want, deep down.

Stuart Wilde, metaphysical writer

The greatest danger for most of us is not that our aim is too high and we miss it, but that it is too low and we reach it.

Michelangelo, Renaissance artist

It takes a person with a mission to succeed.

Clarence Thomas, Supreme Court Justice

Our life is what our thoughts make it.

Marcus Aurelis, Roman emperor

He who wishes to fulfill his mission in the world must be a man of one idea that is, of one great overmastering purpose, overshadowing all his aims and guiding and controlling his entire life.

Julius Bate, English writer

Men, like nails, lose their usefulness when they lose direction and begin to bend.

Walter Savage Landor

Nothing can add more power to your life than concentrating all your energies on a limited set of targets.

Nido Qubein, author and motivational speaker

This one step, choosing a goal and sticking to it, changes everything.

Scott Reed

The mind is the limit. As long as the mind can envision something, you can do it.

Arnold Schwarzenegger, body builder, actor, Governor

If we have our own "why" of life, we can bear almost any "how."
Friedrich Nietzsche, German philosopher

By losing your goal, you have lost your way.
Friedrich Nietzsche, German philosopher

Far away there in the sunshine are my highest aspirations. I may not reach them, but I can look up and see their beauty, believe in them, and try to follow where they lead.
Louisa May Alcott, author

Asking "What if?" questions is not only a lot of fun; it also gives you the freedom to think along different lines.
Roger von Oech, creativity coach

Today's sales should be better than yesterday's—and worse than tomorrow's.
Richard W. Sears, retailer

What is now proved was once only imagined.
William Blake, English poet and painter

The world turns aside to let any man pass who knows whither he is going.
David Starr Jordan, biologist and educator

First, have a definite, clear, practical ideal—a goal, an objective. Second, have the necessary means to achieve your ends—wisdom, money, material and methods. Third, adjust all your means to that end.
Aristotle, Greek philosopher

When you write down your ideas, you automatically focus your full attention on them. Few if any of us can write one thought and think another at the same time. Thus, a pencil and paper make excellent concentration tools.
Michael Leboeuf, business author

Obstacles cannot crush me. Every obstacle yields to stern resolve. He who is fixed to a star does not change his mind.
Leonardo da Vinci, inventor

Lead me to a rock that is too high,
From *Psalms 61:2*

Be careful what you set your heart upon—for it will surely be yours.
James Baldwin, author

Imagination and fiction make up more than three quarters of our real life.
Simon Weil

Obstacles are those frightful things you see when you take your eyes off your goal.
Henry Ford, automotive titan

Set your goals high and don't stop till you get there.
Bo Jackson, professional football and baseball player

The tragedy in life doesn't lie in not reaching your goal. The tragedy lies in having no goal to reach.
Benjamin Mays, clergyman

Goals determine what you're going to be.
Dr. J (Julius Erving), basketball player

If we make up our mind what we are going to make of our lives, then work hard toward that goal, we never lose—somehow we win out.
U.S. President Ronald Reagan, "The Great Communicator"

Not failure, but low aim is crime.
James Russell Lowell, poet and diplomat

Don't be fooled by the calendar. There are only as many days in the year as you make use of. One man gets only a week's value out of a year while another man gets a full year's value out of a week.
Charles Richards

What you are must always displease you if you would attain to that which you are not.
St. Augustine

If thou follow thy star, thou canst not fail of glorious heaven.
> Dante, writer and poet

I decided to be the best and the smartest.
> Oprah Winfrey, actress and media mogul

What the power is I cannot say. All I know is that it exists and it becomes available only when a man is in that state of mind in which he knows exactly what he wants and is fully determined not to quit until he finds it.
> Alexander Graham Bell, inventor

Stretch your foot to the length of your blanket.
> An Old Persian saying

No wind serves him who addresses his voyage to no certain port.
> Montaigne, French writer

Nothing ever built arose to touch the skies unless some man dreamed that it should, some man believed that it could, and some man willed that it must.
> Charles Kettering, inventor

After climbing a great hill, one finds many more hills to climb.
> Nelson Mandela, South African President

Always dream and shoot higher than you know how to. Don't bother just to be better than your contemporaries or predecessors. Try to be better than yourself.
> William Faulkner, author

The will to conquer is the first condition of victory.
> Ferdinand Foch, French military theorist

Mars is there, waiting to be reached.
> Buzz Aldrin, astronaut

High expectation is the key to everything.
> Sam Walton, founder of Wal-Mart

If one is lucky, a solitary fantasy can transform one million realities.
Maya Angelou, poet

I found that when you start thinking and saying what you really want then your mind automatically shifts and pulls you in that direction. And sometimes it can be that simple, just a little twist in vocabulary that illustrates your attitude and philosophy.
Jim Rohn, author and motivational speaker

The reason most people never reach their goals is that they don't define them, or ever seriously consider them as believable or achievable. Winners can tell you where they are going, what they plan to do along the way and who will be sharing the adventure with them.
Denis Watley, success coach and author

You don't have to be a fantastic hero to do certain things—to compete. You can be just an ordinary chap, sufficiently motivated to reach challenging goals.
Edmund Hillary, First to summit Mt. Everest

Goals are dreams with deadlines.
Diana Scharf Hunt, writer

People with goals succeed because they know where they're going.
Earl Nightingale, motivational writer

We are not in a position in which we have nothing to work with. We already have capacities, talents, direction, missions, callings.
Abraham Maslow, psychologist

We hurt ourselves not by what we ask for, but by what we settle for.
Alan Cohen, author

Aim at nothing and you will hit it every time.
Author unknown

If I don't dream that I'll make it, I won't even get close.
Henry Kaiser, industrialist

The past is a guidepost, not a hitching post.
L. Thomas Holdcroft

Whatever course you decide upon, there is always someone to tell you "you are wrong." There are always difficulties arising which tempt you to believe that your critics are right. To map out a course of action and follow it to the end, requires some of the same courage which a soldier needs.
Ralph Waldo Emerson, philosopher

In the long run, men hit only what they aim at.
Henry David Thoreau, author

The secret of success is constancy to purpose.
Benjamin Disraeli, British Prime minister

When you reach for the stars, you may not quite get one, but you won't come up with a handful of mud.
Leo Burnett, advertising executive

Only he who keeps his eye on the far horizon will find his right road.
Dag Hammarskjold, statesman

We succeed only as we identify in life, or war, or in anything else, a single overriding objective, and make all other considerations bend to that one objective.
U.S. President Dwight Eisenhower

Great hopes makes everything great possible.
Benjamin Franklin, statesman

A good goal is like a strenuous exercise, it makes you stretch.
Mary Kay Ash, cosmetic titan

Follow your bliss.
Joseph Campbell, writer and educator

If you believe that someday it's going to happen, someday it probably will happen.

Steve Case, internet executive

Goldfish grow to the size of their tank.

Detective Frank Maloney, NYPD

Chapter 17

Business Planning and Preparation

The 7 P's: Prior, Proper, Planning, Prevents, Piss, Poor, Performance!
David Janke, U.S. Navy Seal Slogan

A good plan today is better than a perfect plan tomorrow.
U.S. General George S. Patton

A good plan violently executed now is better than a perfect plan executed next week.
U.S. General George S. Patton

Prepare for the unknown by studying how others in the past have coped with the unforeseeable and the unpredictable.
U.S. General George S. Patton

Wars are not won by fighting battles: Wars are won by choosing battles.
U.S. General George S. Patton

Look before you leap.
Mom

In action, be primitive; in foresight, a strategist.
Rene Char, French poet

Quick decisions are unsafe decisions.
Sophocles, Greek playwright

It is a bad plan that admits of no modification.
Publilius Syrus, Roman philosopher

You win not by chance, but by preparation.
Roger Maris, baseball player

It is thrifty to prepare today for the wants of tomorrow.
Aesop, Greek philosopher

The time to repair the roof is when the sun is shining.
U.S. President John F. Kennedy

Dig your well before you're thirsty.
Harvey Mackay, author and envelope salesman

It wasn't raining when Noah built the ark.
Harvey Mackay, author and envelope salesman

It's better to be prepared and not have an opportunity than have an opportunity and not be prepared.
Harvey Mackay, author and envelope salesman

Life is what happens to you while you are making other plans.
John Lennon, musician

It is better to look ahead and prepare, than to look back and regret.
Jackie Joyner-Kersee, Olympic runner

Chance favors the prepared mind.
Louis Pasteur, scientist

Our plans miscarry because they have no aim. When one man does not know what harbor he is making for, no wind is the right wind.
Seneca, Roman philosopher

Luck is what happens when preparation meets opportunity.
Seneca, Roman philosopher

If a man does not know to what port he is steering, no wind is favorable to him.
Seneca, Roman philosopher

Better three hours too soon, than a minute too late.
> William Shakespeare, English poet and playwright

People don't plan to fail, they fail to plan.
> Jeff Cain, financial advisor

Leaving the game plan is a sign of panic, and is not in our game plan.
> Chuck Knoll, football coach

The time to worry is before you place the bet, not after the wheel is spinning. Once it spins, you forget about it.
> Bill Parcells, football coach

Everybody has a plan, until they get hit.
> Mike Tyson, former heavyweight champion

I concentrate on preparing to swim my race and let the other swimmers think about me, not me about them.
> Amanda Beard, four time Olympian and model

If you don't know where you're going, you will probably end up somewhere else.
> Laurence Johnson Peter, The Peter Principle

Wealth is the product of man's capacity to think.
> Ayn Rand, author

Plan ahead or find trouble on the doorstep.
> Confucius, Chinese philosopher

Success depends upon previous preparation and without such preparation there is sure to be failure.
> Confucius, Chinese philosopher

Always have a plan and believe it. Nothing happens by accident.
> Chuck Knox, football coach

Every man is the architect of his own fortune.
> Appius Claudius, Roman politician

No wind blows in favor of a ship without a destination.
Author unknown

All you need to succeed is a yellow pad and pencil.
Mark McCormack, first sports agent

Thought is action in rehearsal.
Sigmund Freud, psychiatrist

Winning can be defined as the science of being totally prepared.
George Allen, football coach

Luck is a matter of preparation meeting opportunity.
Oprah Winfrey, actress and media mogul

A discovery is said to be an accident meeting a prepared mind.
Albert Szent-Gyorgi, scientist

Don't expect what you don't expect.
W. Clement Stone, insurance executive and author

Measure twice, cut once.
H. Ross Perot, billionaire

Don't go into the barn without a shovel.
H. Ross Perot, billionaire

Act quickly, think slowly.
Greek Proverb

Deliberate often, decide once.
Latin proverb

My interest is in the future because I am going to spend the rest of my life there.
Charles Kettering, inventor

Don't live in the past, you've already been there.

Author unknown

I dream my painting and then I paint my dream.

Vincent Van Gogh, painter

Chase dear without a guide and you will only go into the forest.

Buddhist saying

It is good to have an end to journey towards; but it is the journey that matters in the end.

Ursula K. LeGuin, novelist and poet

Make no little plans. They have no magic to stir men's blood.

D.B. Hudson, author

No pen, no ink, no table, no room, no time, no quiet, no inclination.

James Joyce, the great Irish author

If there is a 50-50 chance that something can go wrong, then nine times out of ten—it will.

Paul Harvey, radio personality

Need and struggle are what excite and inspire us. Our hour of triumph is what brings the void.

William James, psychologist and philosopher

I do more painting when I'm not painting.

Pablo Picasso, painter

It is when the well is dry that we know the price of water.

Benjamin Franklin, statesman

No enterprise is more likely to succeed than one concealed from the enemy until it is ripe for execution.

Niccolo Machiavelli, Italian political philosopher

We aim above the mark to hit the mark.

Ralph Waldo Emerson, philosopher

The sower may mistake and sow his peas crookedly: the peas make no mistake, but come up and show his line.

Ralph Waldo Emerson, philosopher

It is the eye which makes the horizon.

Ralph Waldo Emerson, philosopher

When defeat comes, accept it as a signal that your plans are not sound. Rebuild those plans and set sail once more toward your coveted goal.

Napoleon Hill, from *Think and Grow Rich*

Do not reveal your thoughts to everyone lest you drive away your good luck.

Apocrypha

A bad beginning makes a bad ending.

Euripides, Greek playwright

It is a mistake to look too far ahead. Only one link of the chain of destiny can be handled at a time.

Sir Winston Churchill, British Prime Minister

The general who wins a battle makes many calculations . . . here the battle is fought. The general who loses a battle makes but a few calculations beforehand.

Sun Tzu, from *The Art of War*

He who is prudent and lies in wait for an enemy who is not, will be victorious

Sun Tzu, from *The Art of War*

Strategy without tactics is the slowest route to victory. Tactics without strategy is the noise before defeat.

Sun Tzu, from *The Art of War*

Victorious warriors win first and then go to war, while defeated warriors go to war first and then seek to win.

Sun Tzu, from *The Art of War*

The loftiest edifices need the deepest foundations.

George Santayana, philosopher and poet

How can a man learn navigation where there's no rudder.

Christopher Fry, English playwright

It is by losing himself in the objective, in inquiry, creation and craft, that a man becomes something.

Paul Goodman, sociologist and writer

The discipline of writing something down is the first step toward making it happen.

Lee Iacocca, automotive executive

The samurai makes one cut but that cut was an entire lifetime in the making.

Richard Templar, writer

I will prepare and someday my chance will come.

U.S. President Abraham Lincoln

The will to win is important, but the will to prepare is vital.

Joe Paterno, football coach

In preparing for battle, I have always found that plans are useless, but planning is indispensable.

U.S. President Dwight Eisenhower

Before everything else, getting ready is the secret of success.

Henry Ford, automotive pioneer

Choice, not chance, determines destiny.

Author unknown

Nothing is more dangerous than an idea when it is the only one you have.

Emile Chartier, French philosopher and journalist

One important key to success is self-confidence. An important key to self-confidence is preparation.

Arthur Ashe, tennis champion

Never underestimate how well you're going to do in life.

Tom Gallagher, attorney

My father always said a fool with a plan will beat a genius with no plan.

T. Boone Pickens, billionaire oilman

The soul cannot think without a picture.

Aristotle, Greek philosopher

Someone's sitting in the shade today because someone planted a seed a long time ago.

Warren Buffet, Investor

Chapter 18

Discipline, Focus and Good Daily Habits

The successful warrior is the average man, with laser-like focus.
Bruce Lee, martial arts expert and actor

No horse gets anywhere until he is harnessed. No stream or gas ever drives anything until it is confined. No Niagara ever turned light and power until it is tunneled. No life ever grows great until it is focused, dedicated, disciplined.
Harry Emerson Fosdick, clergyman

Powerful indeed is the empire of habit.
Publilius Syrus, Roman philosopher

He conquers twice who conquers himself in victory.
Publilius Syrus, Roman philosopher

Continuous effort, not strength or intelligence, is key to unlocking our potential.
Liane Cordes, author

The first and the best victory is to conquer self.
Plato, Greek philosopher

Each man is capable of doing one thing well. If he attempts several, he will fail to achieve distinction in any.
Plato, Greek philosopher

First manage yourself.
Confucius, Chinese philosopher

He who requires much from himself and little from others will keep himself from being the object of resentment.

Confucius, Chinese philosopher

We are what we repeatedly do. Excellence, then, is not an act, but a habit.

Aristotle, Greek philosopher

What it lies in our power to do, it lies in our power not to do.

Aristotle, Greek philosopher

Choose always the way that seems the best, however rough it may be; custom will soon render it easy and agreeable.

Pythagoras, Greek philosopher

I cannot trust a man to control others who cannot control himself.

General Robert E. Lee, Confederate Army

In reading the lives of great men, I found that the first victory they won was over themselves. Self discipline with all of them came first.

U.S. President Harry S. Truman

It is better to conquer yourself than to win a thousand battles. Then the victory is yours. It cannot be taken from you, not by angels or by demons, heaven or hell.

Buddha, founder of Buddhism

Even the gods are moved by the voice of entreaty.

J. Lewis May, author

Pressure is your best friend. It helps you focus on your job, rise earlier, stay later and creates your passion.

Rick Pitino, basketball coach

Rule your mind or it will rule you.

Horace, Roman poet

If you do not conquer self you will be conquered by self.

Napoleon Hill, from *Think and Grow Rich*

If we don't discipline ourselves, the world will do it for us.

William Feather, publisher and author

You never will be the person you can be if pressure, tension and discipline are taken out of your life.

Dr. James G. Bilkey

Not being able to govern events, I govern myself.

Michel de Montaigne, French writer

The only difference between a writer and someone who what to be a writer is discipline.

Ayelet Waldman, author

The secret of discipline is motivation. When a man is sufficiently motivated, discipline will take care of itself.

Sir Alexander Paterson, British Commissioner of Prisons

If you're running a 26 mile marathon, remember that every mile is one step at a time. If you are writing a book, do it one page at a time. If you're trying to master a new language, try it one word at a time. There are 365 days in the average year. Divide any project by 365 and you'll find that no job is all that intimidating. All it takes is discipline—daily discipline, not annual discipline.

Charles Swindoll, clergyman

He who reins within himself and rules passions, desires and fears is more than a king.

John Milton, English poet

Nothing is more harmful to the service than the neglect of discipline; for that discipline, more than numbers, gives one army superiority over another.

U.S. President George Washington

Some people regard discipline as a chore. For me, it is a kind of order that sets me free to fly.

Julie Andrews, actress

One half of life is luck; the other half is discipline and that's the important half, for without discipline you wouldn't know what to do with luck.

Carl Zuckmeyer, writer

Discipline is the bridge between goals and accomplishments.

Jim Rohn, motivational author and speaker

One discipline always leads to another discipline.

Jim Rohn, motivational author and speaker

The successful person has the habit of doing the things failures don't like to do. They don't like doing them either necessarily, but their disliking is subordinated to the strength of their purpose.

E.M. Gray, success author

Discipline yourself to do the things you need to do when you need to do them and the day will come when you will be able to do the things you want to do when you want to do them.

Zig Ziglar, sales trainer and author

Do not consider painful what is good for you.

Euripides. Greek playwright

He who lives without discipline dies without honor.

Icelandic saying

Discipline is remembering what you want.

David Campbell

The only discipline that lasts is self discipline.

Bum Phillips, football coach

Slow and steady wins the race.

From *Aesop's Fables*

When you have a number of disagreeable duties to perform, always do the most disagreeable first.

Josiah Quincy, Revolutionary war soldier

Develop the winning edge; small differences in your performance can lead to large differences in your results.

Brian Tracy, Sales trainer

The secret of success is constancy of purpose.

Benjamin Disraeli, British Prime Minister

Don't look back. Something might be gaining on you.

Satchel Paige, baseball player

Good habits are as addictive as bad habits, and a lot more rewarding.

Harvey Mackay, author and envelope salesman

My life as a writer consists of 1/8th talent and 7/8s discipline.

John Irving, author

Concentration and mental toughness are the margins of victory.

Bill Russell, basketball player

The man who can drive himself further once the effort gets painful is the man who will win.

Roger Banister, runner

First we form habits; then they form us.

Robert Gilbert

There is little that can withstand a man who can conquer himself.

King Louis XIV, ruler of France

The ability to focus attention on important things is a defining characteristic of intelligence.

Dr. Robert Shiller, spiritual leader

Make my joy complete by being of the same mind, maintaining the same love, united in spirit, intent on one purpose.

Philippians 4:2

Any penalty, I've told you a hundred times, can be eliminated by concentration or good judgment.

Bill Parcells, football coach

Success demands singleness of purpose.

Vince Lombardi, football coach

Football is like life—it requires perseverance, self denial, hard work, sacrifice, dedication and respect for authority.

Vince Lombardi, football coach

Winning is not a sometime thing; it's an all time thing. You don't win once in a while, you don't do things right once and a while, you do them right all the time. Winning is a habit. Unfortunately, so is losing.

Vince Lombardi, football coach

The quality of a man's life is in direct proportion to his commitment to excellence.

Tom Landry, football coach

You've got to get up every morning with determination if you're going to go to bed with satisfaction.

George Horace Lorimer, editor and publisher

Chapter 19

Time Management

A small daily task, if it be really daily, will beat the labors of a spasmodic Hercules.

> Anthony Trollope, English novelist

Know the true value of time; snatch, seize, and enjoy every moment of it. No idleness; no laziness; no procrastination; never put off till tomorrow what you can do today.

> Anthony Trollope, English novelist

It's not the daily increase but daily decrease. Hack away at the unessential.

> Bruce Lee, Martial arts expert and actor

The sun has not caught me in bed in fifty years.

> U.S. President Thomas Jefferson

Better three hours too soon, than one minute too late.

> William Shakespeare, English poet and playwright

Lose an hour in the morning and you'll spend all day looking for it.

> Richard Whately, theologian

Never let yesterday use up today.

> Richard H. Nelson, writer

Begin at once to live and count each day as a separate life.

> Seneca, Roman philosopher

Enquire not what boils in another's pot.

> Thomas Fuller, M.D.

Start by doing what is necessary, then do what is possible and suddenly you are doing the impossible.

St. Francis of Assisi

Don't say you don't have enough time. You have exactly the same number of hours per day that were given to Helen Keller, Louis Pasteur, Michelangelo, Leonardo da Vinci, Thomas Jefferson and Albert Einstein.

H. Jackson Brown Jr., author

Don't water your weeds.

Harvey Mackay, author and envelope king

Shape your heart to front the hour, but dream not that the hour will last.

Alfred Lord Tennyson, poet and author

Never try to teach a pig to sing . . . it wastes your time and annoys the pig.

Robert Heinlein, science fiction writer

You control your life by controlling your time.

Conrad Hilton, hotel executive

How you spend your time is more important than how you spend your money. Money mistakes can be corrected, but time is lost forever.

David B. Norris, attorney

Yesterday is not ours to recover, but tomorrow is ours to win or to lose.

U.S. President Lyndon B. Johnson

Perhaps the very best question that you can memorize and repeat, over and over, is "what is the most valuable use of my time right now?"

Brian Tracy, sales coach

Your greatest asset is your earning ability. Your greatest resource is your time.

Brian Tracy, sales coach

A wise person does at once what a fool does at last. Both do the same thing: only at different times.

Baltasar Gracian, Spanish writer

One worthwhile task carried to a successful conclusion is worth half-a-hundred half finished tasks.

Malcolm S. Forbes, Forbes Magazine

The bad news is time flies. The good news is you're the pilot.

Michael Altshuler

A year from now you will wish you had started today.

Karen Lamb, author

Those who make the worst use of their time are the first to complain of its shortness.

Jean de la Bruyere, writer

It's so hard when contemplated in advance and so easy when you do it.

Robert M. Pirsig, writer

Ah—So much time, so little to do.

Willy Wonka, from the movie *Charlie and the Chocolate Factory*

You can't turn back the clock, but you can wind it up again.

Bonnie Prudden, mountaineer

Find a job you like and you add five days to every week.

H. Jackson Brown, Jr., author

Work is a necessity for man—man invented the alarm clock.

Pablo Picasso, painter

Until you value yourself, you will not value your time. Until you value your time, you will not do anything with it.

Dr. M. Scott Peck, author

Realize that now—in this moment of time, you are creating. You are creating your next moment. That is what's real.

Sara Paddison, author

When you have a number of disagreeable duties to perform, always do the most disagreeable first.

Josiah Quincy, revolutionary soldier

Once you have mastered time, you will understand how true it is that most people overestimate what they can accomplish in a year and underestimate what they can achieve in a decade.

Anthony Robbins, success trainer and author

Time flies. It's up to you to be the navigator.

Robert Orben, magician and comedy writer

Time equals life; therefore, waste your time and waste your life, or master your time and master your life.

Alan Lakein, personal time management expert

Failing to plan is planning to fail.

Alan Lakein, personal time management expert

Planning is bringing the future into the present so that you can do something about it now.

Alan Lakein, personal time management expert

Time stays long enough for those who use it.

Leonardo da Vinci, inventor

The essential question is not, "How busy are you?" but, "what are you busy at?" Are you doing what fulfills you?

Oprah Winfrey, actress and media mogul

The average American worker has fifty interruptions a day, of which seventy percent have nothing to do with work.

W. Edwards Deming, business advisor and author

The time you enjoy wasting is not wasted time.

Bertrand Russell, British philosopher and historian

The great dividing line between success and failure can be expressed in five words: I did not have time.

Franklin Field

I'm working to improve my methods and every hour I save is an hour added to my life.

Ayn Rand, author

Time is our most valuable asset, yet we tend to waste it, kill it and spend it rather than invest it.

Jim Rohn, motivational author and speaker

Those who make the worse use of their time are the first to complain of its shortness.

Jean De La Bruyere

It is not enough to be busy, so are ants. The question is what are we busy about?

Henry David Thoreau, writer and philosopher

It's not so much how busy you are, but why you are busy. The bee is praised. The mosquito is swatted.

Mary O'Connor, American novelist

To think too long about doing a thing often becomes its undoing.

Eva Young, author

Learn to differentiate between what is truly important and what can be dealt with at another time.

Mia Hamm, soccer player

The surest way to be late is to have plenty of time.

Leo Kennedy, poet

Does thou love life? Then do not squander time, for that is the stuff life is made of.

Benjamin Franklin, statesman

You may delay, but time will not.

Benjamin Franklin, statesman

Today is worth two tomorrows.

Benjamin Franklin, statesman

Lost time is never found again.

Old Irish proverb

Neither can the wave that has passed by be recalled, nor the hour which has passed return again.

Ovid, Roman poet

If you haven't got the time to do it right, when will you find the time to do it over?

Jeffrey J. Mayer, author of *Time Management for Dummies*

Take care in your minutes and the hours will take care of themselves.

Lord Chesterfield, poet and writer

There is nothing so useless as doing efficiently that which should not be done at all.

Peter Drucker, management expert

Always remember that the future comes one day at a time.

Dean Acheson, secretary of state

The only reason for time is so that everything doesn't happen at once.

Albert Einstein, scientist

Don't agonize. Organize.

Florynce Kennedy, civil rights activist

Many of us spend half our time wishing for things we could have if we didn't spend half our time wishing.

Alexander Woollcott, critic and commentator

It takes time to build a castle.

Irish saying

A minute now is better than a minute later

Author unknown

Today is the tomorrow we worried about yesterday.

Author unknown

Time is the most valuable thing a man can spend.

Diogenes Laetius, Greek philosopher

Time is really the only capital that any human being has and the only capital he can't afford to lose.

Thomas A. Edison, inventor

Nothing is worth more than this day.

Johann Wolfgang von Goethe, German philosopher

We must use time as a tool, not as a crutch.

U.S. President John F. Kennedy

Time and words can't be recalled, even if it was only yesterday.

Yiddish proverb

If you want to make good use of your time, you've got to know what is important and then give it all you've got.

Lee Iacocca, automotive executive

Don't be fooled by the calendar. There are only as many days in the week as you make use of. One man gets only a week's value out of a year while another man gets a full year's value out of a week.

Charles Richards

Live this day as if it will be your last. Remember that you will only find "tomorrow" on the calendars of fools. Forget yesterday's defeat and ignore the problems of tomorrow. This is it. Doomsday. All you have. Make it the best day of your year. The saddest words you can ever utter are, "If I had my life to live over again." Take the baton, now. Run with it! This is your day! Beginning today, treat everyone you meet, friend or foe, loved one or stranger, as if they were going to be dead at midnight. Extend to each person, no matter how trivial the contact, all care and kindness and understanding and love you can muster, and do it with no thought of any reward. Your life will never be the same again.

Og Mandino, motivational writer

It has been my observation that most people get ahead during the time that others waste.

Henry Ford, automotive titan

The older I get, the more wisdom I find in the ancient rule of taking first things first, a process which often reduces the most complex human problems to manageable proportions.

U.S. President Dwight D. Eisenhower

Don't be fooled by the calendar. There are only as many days in the year as you make use of. One man gets only a week's value out of a year while another man gets a full year's value out of a week.

Charles Dow Richards, judge and politician

The man who dares to waste one hour of life has not discovered the value of life.

Charles Darwin, scientist

Chapter 20

Sales Leaders are Team Builders

Even the Lone Ranger didn't do it alone.
> Harvey Mackay, author and envelope king

Innovate, develop, motivate, inspire, trust—be a leader.
> Ted Turner, Media mogul

Manage the golden rule of management: Manage others the way you would like to be managed.
> Brian Tracy, motivational and sales trainer

A pat on the fanny gets you further than a kick in the butt.
> Morris Hite, advertising executive

There is no substitute for talent. Industry and all the virtues are of no avail.
> Aldous Huxley, novelist

If each of us hires people smaller than we are, we shall become a company of dwarfs.
> David Ogilvy, advertising executive

If we were all determined to play the first violin, we should never have an ensemble. Therefore, respect every musician in his proper place.
> Robert Schumann, composer

I don't believe in just ordering people to do things. You have to grab an oar and row with them.
> Harold Geneen, businessman

United we stand, divided we fall.
> George Pope Morris, writer

The whole is more than the sum of its parts.
Aristotle, Greek philosopher

One man can be a crucial ingredient on a team, but one man cannot make a team.
Kareem Abdul-Jabbar, basketball player

An order that can be understood will be understood.
Helmuth von Moltke, soldier

The five steps in teaching an employee new skills are preparation, explanation, showing, observation and supervision.
Bruce Barton, advertising executive

Alone we can do so little; together we can do so much.
Helen Keller, writer and activist

People ask the difference between a leader and a boss . . . The leader works in the open and the boss in covert. The leader leads, and the boss drives.
U.S. President Theodore Roosevelt

There is only one thing worse than fighting with allies, and that is fighting without them.
Sir Winston Churchill, British Prime Minister

You can't help someone get up a hill without getting closer to the top yourself.
H. Norman Schwarzkopf, U.S. Army General

Rain does not fall on one root alone.
Cameroonian proverb

What is not good for the swarm is not good for the bee.
Marcus Aurelius, Roman emperor

No man is an island, entire of itself; every man is a piece of the continent.
John Donne, poet and preacher

We often have to put up with most from those on whom we most depend.

Balthazar Gracian, Spanish writer

For the strength of the pack is the wolf and the strength of the wolf is the pack.

Rudyard Kipling, English writer and poet

You win the victory when you yield to friends.

Sophocles, Greek playwright

Admonish you friends privately, but praise them openly.

Publilius Syrus, Roman philosopher

Anyone can hold the helm when the sea is calm.

Publilius Syrus, Roman Philosopher

The remedy for wrongs is to forget them.

Publilius Syrus, Roman Philosopher

The person who receives the most favors is the one who knows how to return them.

Publilius Syrus, Roman philosopher

Where there is unity there is always victory.

Publilius Syrus, Roman philosopher

Always think of passing the ball before shooting.

John Wooden, basketball coach

The best way to knock the chip off someone's shoulder is to pat him on the back.

Irish saying

I can live for two months on a good compliment.

Mark Twain, American author

And so, fellow Americans, ask not what your county can do for you; ask what you can do for your country.

U.S. President John F. Kennedy

Keep away from people who try to belittle your ambitions. Small people always do that, but the really great make you feel that you too can become great.

Mark Twain, American author

Few things help an individual more than to place responsibility upon him and to let him know that you trust him.

Booker T. Washington, educator

Work is of two kinds: first, altering the position of matter at or near the earth's surface relatively to other such matter; second, telling other people to do so. The first is unpleasant and ill paid; the second is pleasant and highly paid.

Bertrand Russell, from *In Praise of Idleness*

Many people have ideas on how others should change. Few people have ideas on how they should change.

Leo Tolstoy, Russian author

Much silence makes a powerful noise.

African proverb

Give advice; if people don't listen, let adversity teach them.

African saying

Help your brother's boat across, and your own boat will reach the shore.

Hindu proverb

Leaders are visionaries with a poorly developed sense of fear and no concept of the odds against them. They make the impossible happen.

Dr. Robert Jarvik, scientist

If ethics are poor at the top, that behavior is copied down through the organization.

Robert Noyce, Co-founder of Intel Corp

It's not fair to ask others what you are unwilling to do yourself.

Eleanor Roosevelt, first lady

Pay your people the least possible and you'll get from them the same.

Malcolm Forbes, publisher

Feeling gratitude and not expressing it is like wrapping a present and not giving it.

William Arthur Ward, educator

Teaching of others teacheth the teacher.

Thomas Fuller, M.D.

Eagles don't flock—you have to find them one at a time.

Ross Perot, billionaire

You can't treat your people like an expense item.

Andy Grove, co-founder of Intel Corporation

Catch people doing things right! Then tell everyone about it.

Ken Blanchard, motivational and business author

I have yet to find the man, however exalted his station, who did not do better work and put forth greater effort under a spirit of approval than under a spirit of criticism.

Charles M. Schwab, steel titan

Lots of people want to ride with you in the limo, but what you want is someone who will take the bus with you when the limo breaks down.

Oprah Winfrey, actor and media mogul

Finding good players is easy. Getting them to play as a team is another story.

Casey Stengel, baseball manager

Management is nothing more than motivating other people.

Lee Iacocca, CEO of Chrysler

When I give a man an office, I watch him carefully to see whether he is swelling or growing.

U.S. President Woodrow Wilson

If anything goes bad, I did it. If anything goes semi-good, we did it. If anything goes really good, then you did it. That's all it takes to get people to win football games for you.
Bear Bryant, football coach

Tact is the ability to describe others as they see themselves.
U.S. President Abraham Lincoln

Many hands make light work.
John Heywood, English writer and playwright

I not only use all the brains I have, but all that I can borrow.
U.S. President Woodrow Wilson

Kindness is more important than wisdom, and recognition of this is the beginning of wisdom.
Theodore Isaac Rubin, M.D.

Difference of opinion leads to inquiry, and inquiry to truth.
U.S. President Thomas Jefferson

We must all hang together, or assuredly we shall all hand separately.
Benjamin Franklin, statesman

You can discover more about a person in an hour of play than in a year of conversation.
Plato, Greek philosopher

Coming together is a beginning. Keeping together is progress. Working together is success.
Henry Ford, automotive giant

I cannot teach anybody anything; I can only make them think.
Socrates, Greek philosopher

A superior man blames himself. The inferior man blames others.
Don Shula, football coach

A true leader inspires others to lead themselves.
> Ari Kaplan, executive

Nothing so consciously proves a man's ability to lead others as what he does from day to day to lead himself.
> Thomas J. Watson Sr., founder of IBM

If I have seen farther than others, it is because I was standing on the shoulder of giants.
> Sir Isaac Newton, scientist

I suppose leadership at one time meant muscles, but today it means getting along with people.
> Mahatma Gandhi, spiritual and political leader of India

A real friend is one who walks in, when the rest of the world walks out.
> Walter Winchell, newspaper and radio personality

Young man, the secret of my success is that at an early age I discovered I was not God.
> Oliver Wendell Holmes, Jr., Supreme Court Justice

Light is the task where many share the toll.
> Homer, Greek writer

It takes no genius to observe that a one man band never gets very big.
> Charles A. Garfield, author

There are no problems we cannot solve together and very few that we can solve by ourselves.
> George B. Johnson, science writer

Lead, follow or get out of the way.
> Thomas Paine, revolutionist

Example is the best precept.
> Aesop, Greek philosopher

Union gives strength.

Aesop, Greek philosopher

United we stand; divided we fall.

Aesop, Greek philosopher

Surround yourself with the best people you can find, delegate authority and don't interfere.

U.S. President Ronald Reagan, *The Great Communicator*

If I accept you as you are, I will make you worse; however if I treat you as though you are what you are capable of becoming, I help you become that.

Johann Wolfgang von Goethe, German poet and writer

Chapter 21

Decide and Take Action Now!

Whatever you think you can do or believe you can do, begin it, for action has magic, grace and power in it.

Johann Wolfgang von Goethe, German philosopher

Knowing is not enough; we must apply. Willing is not enough; we must do.

Johann Wolfgang von Goethe, German philosopher

Until one is committed, there is hesitancy; the chance to draw back; always ineffectiveness concerning all acts of initiative and creation. There is one elemental truth, the ignorance of which kills countless ideas and splendid plans: that the moment one commits oneself, Providence moves all. All sorts of things occur to help one that would never otherwise have occurred. A whole stream of events issue from the decision, raising in one's favor all manner of incidents and meetings and material assistance which no one could have dreamed would come his or her way.

Johann Wolfgang von Goethe, German philosopher

Rest not! Life is sweeping by. Go and dare before you die.

Johann Wolfgang von Goethe, German philosopher

A good beginning makes a good ending.

English saying

The journey of a thousand miles must begin with the first step.

Chinese proverb

The first step is half the distance.

Indian proverb

In the arena of human life the honours and rewards fall to those who show their good qualities in action.

Aristotle, Greek philosopher

He who hesitates is poor!

Mel Brooks, director and producer

Just do it!

Nike Company Slogan

Decide that you want it more than you are afraid of it.

Bill Cosby, comedian and actor

The shortest answer is doing.

British proverb

The beginning is the most important part of the work.

Plato, Greek philosopher

Well done is better than well said.

Benjamin Franklin, statesman

The Constitution only gives people the right to pursue happiness. You have to catch it yourself.

Benjamin Franklin, statesman

Do nothing and nothing happens. Do something and something happens.

Benjamin Franklin, statesman

The problem with doing nothing is not knowing when you're finished.

Benjamin Franklin, statesman

You may delay, but time will not.

Benjamin Franklin, statesman

Never leave till tomorrow which you can do today.

Benjamin Franklin, statesman

Up, sluggard, and waste not life; in the grave will be sleeping enough.

Benjamin Franklin, statesman

Whatever you can do, or dream you can, begin it! Boldness has genius, power and magic in it.

Johann Wolfgang von Goethe, German philosopher

A bold onset is half the battle.

Giuseppe Garibaldi, soldier

An ounce of action is worth a ton of theory.

Friedrich Engels, philosopher and economist

Talk does not cook rice.

Chinese saying

Life is just a blank slate, what matters is what you write on it.

Christine Frankland

When you pray, move your feet.

Quaker saying

Words without action are the assassins of idealism.

U.S. President Herbert Hoover

What you lack in talent can be made up with desire, hustle and giving 110% all the time.

Don Zimmer, baseball coach

If not now, when?

A good psychologist

Motion creates emotion.

Anthony Robbins, success trainer and author

The secret to success is massive failure.

Anthony Robbins, success trainer and author

Massive failure is the secret to massive success.

Anthony Robbins, success trainer and author

One that would have the fruit must climb the tree.

Thomas Fuller, M.D., clergyman and historian

Nothing is easy to the unwilling.

Thomas Fuller, M.D., clergyman and historian

Either move or be moved.

Colin Powell, Secretary of State and U.S. General

There is nothing more powerful than an idea whose time has come.

Victor Hugo, writer

There are only three colors, ten digits and seven notes. It's what we do with them that's important.

Ruth Ross, writer

You miss 100% of the shots you never take.

Wayne Gretzky, hockey Player

My motto was always to keep swinging. Whether I was in a slump of feeling badly or having trouble off the field, the only thing to do was keep swinging.

Hank Aaron, baseball player

Light tomorrow with today.

Elizabeth Barrett Browning, writer

Act quickly, think slowly.

Greek Proverb

No task is a long one but the task on which one dare not start. It becomes a nightmare.

Charles Baudelaire, author

How wonderful it is that nobody need wait a single moment before starting to improve the world.

Anne Frank, diarist

A committee is a cul-de-sac down which ideas are lured and quietly strangled.

Sir Barnett Cocks, British statesman

If you think too long, you think wrong.

Jim Kaat, baseball player

If you wish to reach the highest, begin at the lowest.

Publilius Syrus, Roman philosopher

Audacity augments courage; hesitation, fear.

Publilius Syrus, Roman philosopher

No one knows what he can do until he tries.

Publilius Syrus, Roman philosopher

Valor grows by daring, fear by holding back.

Publilius Syrus, Roman philosopher

While we stop to think, we often miss our opportunity.

Publilius Syrus, Roman philosopher

I didn't get where I am by thinking about it or dreaming it. I got there by doing it.

Estee Lauder, cosmetic entrepreneur

To think too long about doing a thing often becomes its undoing.

Eva Young, author

Of all the sad words of tongue or pen, the saddest are these: "It might have been."

John Greenleaf Whittier, poet and abolitionist

You can either be part of the steamroller or part of the pavement.

David Wanetick, business writer

The joy of life is to put out one's power in some natural and useful or harmless way. There is no other. And the real misery is not to do this.

Oliver Wendell Holmes, U.S. Supreme Court Justice

One of these days is none of these days.

English proverb

Procrastination is the thief of time.

Edward Young, English poet

Do your duty and leave the rest to the gods.

Pierre Corneille, French playwright

The secret of being miserable is to have leisure to bother about whether you are happy or not.

George Bernard Shaw, Irish playwright

A life spent making mistakes is not only more honorable, but more useful than a life spent doing nothing.

George Bernard Shaw, Irish playwright

If you take too long in deciding what to do with your life, you'll find you've done it.

George Bernard Shaw, Irish playwright

Go wake up your luck!

Persian proverb

Expect poison from standing water.

William Blake, psychologist

A rolling stone gathers no moss.

Old English proverb

Live your life so that even if you lose, you will be ahead.

Will Rogers, humorist and comedian

Even if you're on the right track, you'll get run over if you just sit there.

Will Rogers, humorist and comedian

I'd rather die on my feet than live on my knees!

Jerome Messana, the quintessential power salesperson

He who waits upon fortune is never sure of dinner.

Chinese proverb

Iron rusts from disuse; stagnant water loses its purity and in cold weather becomes frozen; even so does inaction sap the vigor of the mind.

Leonardo da Vinci, inventor

Let your hook be always cast for in the pool where you least expect it will be fish.

Ovid, Roman poet

Life is now shitbird—not two years from now when you're making a gazillion dollars—it's right now!

David Janke, U.S. Navy Seal and Wall Street Powerbroker

You don't' get to choose how you're going to die, or when. You can only decide how you're going to live. Now!

Joan Baez. Folk singer

I am seeking; I am striving; I am in it with all my heart.

Vincent Van Gogh, painter

The future comes one day at a time.

Dean Acheson, statesman and lawyer

The future is purchased by the present.

Samuel Johnson, English author and journalist

One must learn by doing the thing, for though you think you know it, you have no certainty until you try.
Success, remember is the reward of toil.

Sophocles, Greek playwright

Success is dependent on effort.
> Sophocles, Greek playwright

Success, remember is the reward of toil.
> Sophocles, Greek playwright

Success is dependent on effort.
> Sophocles, Greek playwright

An idle mind is the devils workshop.
> Old adage

Genius is the ability to put into effect what is in your mind.
> F. Scott Fitzgerald, writer

It's so hard when contemplated in advance and so easy when you do it.
> Robert Pirsig, writer and philosopher

The time when you need to do something is when no one else is willing to do it—when people are saying it can't be done.
> Will Durant, writer

If we did all the things we are capable of doing, we would literally astound ourselves.
> Thomas Alva Edison, inventor

If you want to increase your success ratio, double your failure rate.
> Thomas Watson, Sr., founder of IBM

If one is too lazy to think, too vain to do a thing badly, too cowardly to admit it, one will never attain wisdom.
> Cyril Connolly, English writer and critic

The surest way to go broke is to sit around waiting for a break.
> Author unknown

The future has waited long enough, if we do not grasp it, other hands, grasping hard and bloody will.
> Adlai Stevenson, politician

In the arena of human life the honours and rewards fall to those who show their qualities in action.

Aristotle, Greek philosopher

With regard to excellence, it is not enough to know, but we must try to have and use it.

Aristotle, Greek philosopher

Each of us has a finite number of heartbeats—a finite number of seconds—a finite number of minutes—a finite number of years. Why then, are we so nonchalant about killing time? When we waste time, we waste life. When we kill time, we kill our own lives. If life is precious, then so is time and we can not waste a moment of it.

Pat Williams, Orlando Magic

Life is like riding a bicycle—you don't fall of unless you stop peddling.

Claude Pepper, U.S. Senator

A business, like an automobile, has to be driven in order to get results.

B.C. Forbes, publisher

A good beginning makes a good ending.

English proverb

An ounce of action is worth a ton of theory.

Friedrich Engels, German philosopher and scientist

Go wake up your luck.

A Persian proverb

How much of human life is lost in waiting.

Ralph Waldo Emerson, philosopher

What you do speaks so loudly that I cannot hear what you say.

Ralph Waldo Emerson, philosopher

Progress is the activity of today and the assurances of tomorrow.

Ralph Waldo Emerson, philosopher

Practice is nine-tenths.
Ralph Waldo Emerson, philosopher

No matter how much faculty of idle seeing a man has, the step from knowing to doing is rarely taken.
Ralph Waldo Emerson, philosopher

People who know how to act are never preachers.
Ralph Waldo Emerson, philosopher

To fill the hour—that is happiness.
Ralph Waldo Emerson, philosopher

All life is an experiment. The more experiments you make the better.
Ralph Waldo Emerson, philosopher

Half the agony of living is waiting.
Alexander Rose, author and historian

Would you like me to give you a formula for success? It's quite simple, really: Double your rate of failure. You are thinking of failure as the enemy of success. But it isn't at all. You can be discouraged by failure—or you can learn from it. So go ahead and make mistakes. Make all you can. Because remember that's where you will find success.
Thomas J. Watson Sr., IBM founder

Things may come to those who wait, but only the things left by those who hustle.
U.S. President Abraham Lincoln

A wise person does at once what a fool does at last. Both do the same thing, only at different times.
John Dalberg Acton, historian

Talent is like a faucet; while it is open, you have to write. Inspiration? A hoax fabricated by poets for their self importance.
Jean Anouilh, dramatist

Once men are caught up in an event, they cease to be afraid. Only the unknown frightens men.

Antoine de Saint-Exupery, aviator and writer

The first step is half the distance.

Indian proverb

They who lack talent expect things to happen without effort. They ascribe failure to a lack of education or inspiration or ability, or to misfortunes, rather than to insufficient application. At the core of every true talent there is an awareness of the difficulties inherent in any achievement, and the confidence that by persistence and patience, something worthwhile will be realized. Thus, talent is a species of vigor.

Eric Hoffer, philosopher and longshoreman

Do or do not. There is no try.

Yoda, the Jedi Master in the movie *Star Wars*

All glory comes from daring to begin.

Alexander Graham Bell, scientist

Only those who dare to fail miserably can achieve greatly.

U.S. Senator Robert F. Kennedy

The way to get started is to quit talking and begin doing.

Walt Disney, entertainment mogul

In any moment of decision the best thing you can do is the right thing, the next best thing is the wrong thing, and the worst thing you can do is nothing.

U.S. President Theodore Roosevelt

The world is not dangerous because of those who do harm but because of those who look at it without doing anything.

Albert Einstein, scientist

If one advances confidently in the direction of his dreams and endeavors to live the life he has imagined, he will meet with success unexpected in common hours.

Henry David Thoreau, writer and philosopher

Inaction may be the biggest form of action.

Jerry Brown, Governor of California

A great flame follows a little spark.

Dante Alighieri, poet

In great attempts, it is glorious even to fail.

Longinus, writer

In life, be a participant, not a spectator.

Lou Holtz, football coach

WD-40 Oil: the name of the company came from the amount of times, years and toil it took the founder to perfect the number one selling machine oil in the world: Water Displacement on the 40th try.

Author unknown

Our nature consists in motion; complete rest is death.

W.F. Trotter, author

The secret of success is to do the common things uncommonly well.

John D. Rockefeller, oil magnate

I hear and I forget. I see and I remember. I do and I understand.

Confucius, Chinese philosopher

Action, alone, is the tinder which ignites the map, the parchment, this scroll, my dreams, my plans, my goals, into a living force. Action is the food and drink which will nourish my success.

Og Mandino, motivational author

It is better to act and fail than not to act and flounder.

Og Mandino, motivational author

I myself must mix with action, lest I wither by despair.
Lord Alfred Tennyson, poet

Our company has indeed stumbled onto some of its new products. But you can only stumble if you're moving.
Richard Carlton, former CEO of 3M Corporation

Failure is not our only punishment for laziness: there is also the success of others.
Jules Renard, French author

Waiting for a great idea is a bad idea.
Henry Ford, automotive titan

Action will remove the doubt that theory cannot solve.
Chinese saying

The first man gets the oyster; the second man gets the shell.
Andrew Carnegie, steel magnate

The average person puts only 25% of his energy and ability into his work. The world takes off its hat to those who put in more than 50% of their capacity and stands on its head for those few and far between souls who devote 100%.
Andrew Carnegie, steel magnate

However, much thou art read in theory, if thou has no practice, thou art ignorant.
Sa'di, Persian poet

This is the precious moment, but strangely, few people know it.
Timothy Miller, psychologist

If not now, when?
Author unknown

It's a sad day when you find out that it's not an accident, or time or fortune, but just yourself that kept things from you.

Lillian Hellman, playwright

Everyone who's ever taken a shower has an idea. It's the person who gets out of the shower, dries off and does something about it who makes a difference.

Nolan Bushnell, executive

The past exists only in our memories, the future only in our plans. The present is our only reality.

Robert Pirsig, author

We are all failures—at least, all the best of us are.

Sir James Matthew Barrie, Scottish novelist

Look at a day when you are supremely satisfied at the end: It's not a day when you lounge around doing nothing; it's when you've had everything to do and you've done it.

Margaret Thatcher, British Prime Minister

Action may not always bring happiness; but there is no happiness without action.

Benjamin Disraeli, British statesman

If you hear a voice within you saying, "You are not a painter," then by all means paint and that voice will be silenced.

Vincent Van Gogh, painter

The credit belongs to the man who is actually in the arena, whose face is marred by dust and sweat and blood, who strives valiantly; who errs and comes short again and again, who knows the great enthusiasms, the great devotions, and spends himself in a worthy cause; who at best knows the triumph of high achievement; and who, at worst, if he fails, at least fails while daring greatly, so that his place shall never been with those cold and timid souls who know neither victory nor defeat.

U.S. President Theodore Roosevelt

It is not because things are difficult that we do not dare, it is because we do not dare that they are difficult.

> Seneca, Roman philosopher

The profit on a good action is to have done it.

> Seneca, Roman philosopher

Hard work spotlights the character of people: some turn up their sleeves, some turn up their noses and some don't turn up at all.

> Sam Ewig, author

The world is so fast that there are days when the person who says, "It can't be done," is interrupted by the person who is doing it.

> Harry Emerson Fosdick, clergyman

It is vain to expect our prayers to be heard if we do not strive as well as pray

> Aesop, Greek philosopher

A rolling stone gathers no moss.

> Old British saying

**What if Columbus had been told, "Chris baby, don't go now. Wait until we've solved our
Number one priorities—war and famine, poverty and crime, pollution and disease, illiteracy and racial hatred.**

> Bill Gates, founder of Microsoft

Cessation of work is not accompanied by a cessation of expenses.

> Cato the Elder, Roman statesman

When you come to a fork in the road—take it!

> Yogi Berra, baseball player, manager

Fools look to tomorrow; wise men use tonight.

> Scottish Proverb

Life is not lost dying; life is lost minute by minute, day by dragging day, in all the thousand small uncaring ways.

Stephen Vincent Benet, poet and novelist

Time is really the only capital that any human being has and the only thing he can't afford to lose.

Thomas Edison, inventor

A thousand things advance; nine hundred and ninety-nine retreat: that is progress.

Henri-Frederic Amiel, Swiss philosopher and poet

The shortest way to do many things is to do only one thing at once.

Samuel Smiles, Scottish author and reformer

Repetition is the mother of skill.

Old teaching adage

Either dance well or quit the ballroom.

Greek proverb

Do it. That's what it's all about: any man who wants can produce a good boat. It takes some study, some practice, and, of course, experience. The experience starts coming the minute you begin and not one jot before. I sometimes hear the wail, "I have no experience." Start. Start anything and experience comes. As one of my friends says, "It's only a boat; go ahead and build it." If the first effort is a bit lumpy, so what? There will be another much less lumpy later on.

R.D. Culler, maritime author

Never let the fear of striking out get in your way.

Babe Ruth, homerun king

It's a mere moment in a man's life between an All-Star Game and an Old-Timer's game.

Vince Scully, sportscaster

The "How" thinker gets problems solved effectively because he wastes no time with futile "Ifs."

Dr. Norman Vincent Peale, spiritual leader

Waste no time arguing what a good man should be—be one!

Marcus Aurelius, Roman Emperor

Whether it's the best of times or the worst of times, it's the only time we've got.

Art Buchwald, writer and humorist

Sooner or later are not days of the week.

Greg Hickman, motivational writer

Everything comes to him who hustles while he waits.

Thomas Edison, inventor

The great end of life is not knowledge, but action.

Thomas Henry Huxley, biologist

It is better to wear out than to rust out.

Richard Cumberland, philosopher

It's better to burnout than to fade away.

Neil Young, songwriter and poet

Once begun, a task is easy; half the work is done.

Horace, Roman poet

A good beginning makes a good ending.

English proverb

Our birth is nothing but our death begun.

Edward Young, English poet

All things are difficult before they are easy.

Thomas Fuller, M.D.

Do not consider painful what is good for you.
> Euripides, Greek playwright

Leave no stone unturned.
> Euripides, Greek playwright

Much effort, much prosperity.
> Euripides, Greek playwright

The future has waited long enough; if we do not grasp it, other hands, grasping hard and bloody will.
> Adlai Stevenson, politician and diplomat

It is better to light a candle than curse the darkness.
> Chinese proverb

The devil tempts all other men, but idle men tempt the devil.
> Turkish proverb

Idleness is a mother. She has a son, robbery and a daughter, hunger.
> Victor Hugo, French poet and playwright

The worst pain a man can have is to know much and be impotent to act.
> Herodotus, Greek historian

You can't build a reputation on what you're going to do.
> Henry Ford, automotive titan

You don't have to see the top of the staircase to take the first step.
> Martin Luther King, Jr., civil rights leader

Name the greatest of all the inventors—accident!
> Mark Twain, American author

If you're out playing in traffic—you're going to get hit!
> Old selling adage

Things may come to those who wait, but only what's left behind by those who hustle.

U.S. President Abraham Lincoln

I am not built for academic writings. Action is my domain.

Mahatma Gandhi, spiritual and political leader of India

Industry is a better horse to ride than genius.

Walter Lippmann, journalist

Never mistake motion for action.

Ernest Hemingway, author

He who hesitates is a damned fool.

Mae West, actress

Do not confuse motion and progress. A rocking horse keeps moving, but does not make any progress.

Alfred Montapert, writer

The past cannot be changed. The future is yet in your power.

Mark Pickford, actor

When you cannot make up your mind which of two evenly balanced courses of action you should take, choose the bolder.

W.J. Slim, warrior

It's all right to hesitate if you then go ahead.

Bertolt Brecht, German poet and playwright

You can't build a reputation on what you are going to do.

Henry Ford, automotive titan

Action is the fundamental key to all success.

Pablo Picasso, painter

Keep your eyes open and get on with it.
Sir Laurence Olivier, actor and director

What would you attempt to do if you knew you could not fail?
Dr. Robert Schuller, spiritual leader

It's never too late to be what you might have been.
George Eliot, English novelist

Start where you are.
Indian saying

Don't judge each day by the harvest you reap, but by the seeds you plant.
Robert Louis Stevenson, Scottish novelist and poet

The road to success is lined with many tempting parking spaces.
Author unknown

In our era, the road to holiness necessarily passes through the world of action.
Dag Hammarskjold, United Nations President

There are three kinds of people: Those who make things happen, those who watch things happen, and those who ask, "What happened?"
Casey Stengel, baseball manager

He that has done nothing has known nothing.
Thomas Carlyle, from *Corn-Law Rhymes*

If we wait for the moment when everything, absolutely everything, is ready, we shall never begin.
Ivan Turgenev, Russian novelist

Let him that would move the world, first move himself.
Socrates, Greek philosopher

To do is to be.
Socrates, Greek philosopher

If you stop every time a dog barks, your road will never end.

Arabian proverb

In playing ball, or in life, a person occasionally gets the opportunity to do something great. When that time comes, only two things matter: being prepared to seize the moment and having the courage to take your best swing.

Henry Aaron, baseball player

When it comes to getting things done, we need fewer architects and more brick layers.

Colleen C. Barrett, airline executive

There is nothing in the middle of the road but yellow stripes and dead armadillos.

John Hightower

The test of any man lies in action.

Pindar, Greek poet

In all your endeavors, strive to position yourself in the center of the whirlpool.

Kazuo, entrepreneur

There are three ways you can get to the top of a tree: sit on an acorn; makes friends with a bird; climb it.

Author unknown

The person who says it cannot be done should not interrupt the person doing it.

Chinese Proverb

Start where you are. Use what you have. Do what you can.

Arthur Ashe, tennis player

I don't believe in a fate that will fall on us no matter what we do. I do believe in a fate that will fall on us if we do nothing.

U.S. President Ronald Reagan, *The Great Communicator*

Yesterday is history. Tomorrow is a mystery. And today? Today is a gift. That's why we call it the present.

        B Olatunji, musician

Each morning sees some task begun, each evening sees it close; something attempted, something done, has earned a night's repose.

        Henry Wadsworth Longfellow, poet

When you were born, you cried and the world rejoiced. Live your life so that when you die, the world cries and you rejoice.

        Cherokee Indian saying

Unreal is action without discipline, charity without sympathy, ritual without devotion.

        Bhagavad Gita, sacred Indian scripture

Action speaks louder than coaches.

        Speedo advertisement

Never mistake activity for achievement.

        John Wooden, basketball coach

The body moves naturally, automatically, without any personal intervention or awareness. If we think too much, our actions become slow and hesitant.

        Taisen Deshimaru, Zen Buddhist teacher

A life of reaction is a life of slavery, intellectually and spiritually. One must fight for a life of action, not reaction.

        Rita Mae Brown, writer

A decision is the action an executive must take when he has information so incomplete that the answer does not suggest itself.

        U.S. Admiral Arthur Radford, U.S. Navy

Grip it and rip it!

        John Daly, professional golfer

Success seems to be connected with action. Successful people keep moving. They make mistakes, but they don't quit.

Conrad Hilton, hotel entrepreneur

Somebody should tell us, right at the start of our lives that we are dying. Then we might live life to the limit, every minute of every day. Do it! I say. Whatever you want to do, do it now! There are only so many tomorrows.

Michael Landon, actor and director

You don't have to be great to start, but you have to start to be great.

Zig Ziglar, sales trainer

Chapter 22

Take Risks and Make Mistakes!

Leap and the net will appear.
> Julia Cameron, artist and writer

Risk the fall in order to fly.
> Karen Goldman, writer

Behold the turtle. He makes progress when he sticks his neck out.
> James Conant, chemist

The meek shall inherit the earth, but not the mineral rights.
> John Paul Getty, oil billionaire

If the lion didn't bite the tamer every once and awhile, it wouldn't be exciting.
> Darrell Waltrip, racecar driver

Far better it is to dare mighty things, to win glorious triumphs even though checkered by failure, than to rank with those timid spirits who neither enjoy nor suffer much because they live in the gray twilight that knows neither victory nor defeat.
> U.S. President Theodore Roosevelt

The Boogieman doesn't have that many boogies!
> Donny Deutsch, advertising mogul and television host

Fortune favors the bold.
> Virgil, Roman poet

People fail forward to success.
> Mary Kay Ash, cosmetic titan

You can't steal second base and keep your foot on first.

Frederick Wilcox, writer

Whenever you see a successful business, someone once made a courageous decision.

Peter Drucker, author and management consultant

What is more mortifying than to feel that you have missed the plum for want of courage to shake the tree?

Logan Pearsall Smith, writer and critic

Why not go out on a limb? Isn't that where the fruit is?

Frank Scully, author

Do the thing you fear and the death of that fear is certain.

Ralph Waldo Emerson, philosopher

Don't be too timid or squeamish about your actions. All life is an experiment. The more you make, the better.

Ralph Waldo Emerson, philosopher

Do not go where the path may lead, go instead where there is no path and leave a trail.

Ralph Waldo Emerson, philosopher

We must walk consciously only part way toward our goal, and then leap in the dark to our success.

Henry David Thoreau, writer and philosopher

None but the brave deserves the fair.

John Dryden, English poet

Courage is a kind of salvation.

Plato, Greek philosopher

It's not brave unless you're scared.

Author unknown

In great attempts it is glorious even to fail.
> Vince Lombardi, football coach

If you can't accept losing, you can't win.
> Vince Lombardi, football coach

One man with courage makes a majority.
> U.S. President Andrew Jackson

Only those who dare to fail miserably can achieve greatly.
> U.S. Senator Robert F. Kennedy

He who doesn't risk never gets to drink the champagne.
> Russian Proverb

All of life is the management of risk, not its elimination.
> Walter Wriston, banking executive

Be bold. If you're going to make an error, make a doozy, and don't be afraid to hit the ball.
> Billie Jean King, tennis player

I think that only daring speculation can lead us further and not accumulation of facts.
> Albert Einstein, scientist

Anyone who has never made a mistake has never tried anything new.
> Albert Einstein, scientist

Unless you enter the tigers den . . . you cannot take the cubs.
> Japanese saying

If you want to increase your success rate, double your failure rate.
> Thomas Watson Sr., founder of IBM

Don't listen to those who say you're taking too big a chance. Michelangelo would have painted the Sistine floor and it would surely be rubbed out by today.
> Neil Simon, playwright

Life is either a daring adventure or nothing.

Helen Keller, author

Some days you tame the tiger. And some days the tiger has you for lunch.

Tug McGraw, New York Mets relief pitcher

You try to be greedy when others are fearful and fearful when others are greedy.

Warren Buffet, investor

It is courage, courage, courage that raises the blood of life to crimson splendor.

George Bernard Shaw, Irish playwright

This will remain the land of the free only so long as it is the home of the brave.

Elmer Davis, news reporter and author

There's nothing in the middle-of-the-road but yellow strips and dead armadillos.

James Hightower, syndicated columnist

We have more ability than willpower and it's often an excuse to ourselves that we imagine things that are impossible.

La Rochefoucauld, French author

Yesterday is not ours to recover, but tomorrow is ours to win or lose.

U.S. President Lyndon B. Johnson

I'd rather be a could-be if I cannot be an are; because a could-be is a maybe who is reaching for a star. I'd rather be a has-been than a might-have-been, by far; for a might have been has never been, but a has was once an are.

Milton Berle, comedian

Faith is to believe what you do not see . . . the reward for this faith is to see what you believe.

St. Augustine

Experience is the name everyone gives to their mistakes.
Oscar Wilde, Irish author

It doesn't mean anything unless you're nervous and two, always, always be ready.
Tito Puente, musician

Courage is not the lack of fear. It is acting in spite of it.
Mark Twain, American author

Twenty years from now, you will be more disappointed by the things you didn't do than the ones you did. So throw off the bowlines. Sail away from the safe harbor. Catch the trade wind in your sails. Explore. Dream. Discover.
Mark Twain, American author

The time when you need to do something is when no one else is willing to do it, when people are saying it can't be done.
Will Durant, historian

Never believe that a few caring people can't change the world. For, indeed, that's all who ever have.
Margaret Mead, cultural anthropologist

What would life be if we had no courage to attempt anything?
Vincent van Gogh, painter

Keep your fears to yourself, but share your courage with others.
Robert Louis Stevenson, writer

One man with courage makes a majority.
U.S. President Andrew Jackson

Fear is your best friend or your worst enemy. It's like fire. If you can control it, it can cook for you; it can heat your house. If you can't control it, it will burn everything around you and destroy you.
Cus D'Amato, boxing trainer

He who fears something gives it power over him.
Moorish saying

It is better to be a lion for a day than a sheep all your life.

Elizabeth Kenny, nurse

No balls, no blue chips!

Carl Mather, executive recruiter

Failure is good. It's fertilizer. Everything I've learned about coaching I've learned from making mistakes.

Rick Pitino, basketball coach

Nothing is more expensive than a missed opportunity.

H. Jackson Brown Jr., author

Courage is fear holding on a minute longer.

U.S. General George S. Patton

Take calculated risks. That is quite different from being rash.

U.S. General George S. Patton

Put'em up—Put'em up!

The Cowardly Lion, from *The Wizard of OZ*

Never let the fear of striking out get in your way.

Babe Ruth, homerun king

A just cause is not ruined by a few mistakes.

Feodor Dostoyevsky, Russian author

Failure is the condiment that gives success its flavor.

Truman Capote, writer

Don't worry about the world coming to and end today—it's already tomorrow in Australia.

Charles Schulz, cartoonist

Growth demands a temporary surrender of security.

Gail Sheehy, writer

Great faith will always lose out to great faith.
Zig Ziglar, motivational writer

Life is either a daring adventure, or nothing.
Helen Keller, author and activist

The greatest mistake you can make in life is to be continually fearing that you will make one.
Elbert Hubbard, writer

Don't play for safety. It's the most dangerous thing in the world.
Sir Hugh Seymour Walpole, English novelist

If you don't risk anything, you risk even more.
Erica Jong, writer

The only limit to our realization of tomorrow will be our doubts of today.
U.S. President Franklin D. Roosevelt

You must do the very thing you think you cannot do.
Eleanor Roosevelt, First Lady

We must do that which we think we cannot.
Eleanor Roosevelt, First Lady

You may be disappointed if you fail, but you are doomed if you don't try.
Beverly Sills, Operatic soprano

They never fail who die in a great cause.
Lord George Gordon Byron, English poet

You've got to jump off cliffs all the time and build your wings on the way down.
Ray Bradbury, writer

It is courage, courage, courage that raises the blood of life to crimson splendor.
George Bernard Shaw, Irish playwright

Cowards die many times before their deaths. The valiant never taste of death but once.

William Shakespeare, English poet and playwright

Our doubts are traitors and make us lose the good we often might win by fearing to attempt.

William Shakespeare, English poet and playwright

Danger and delight grow on one stalk.

English proverb

Everything is sweetened by risk.

Alexander Smith

If everything seems under control, you're just not going fast enough.

Mario Andretti, car racer

Fortune sides with him who dares.

Virgil, Roman poet

Fortune is not on the side of the faint-hearted.

Sophocles, Greek playwright

He that lives upon hope will die upon fasting.

Benjamin Franklin, statesman

The best brewer sometimes makes bad beer.

German proverb

Half the failures in life arise from pulling in one's horse as he is leaping.

Augustus William Hare, British writer and cleric

We are all, in some sense, mountaineers.

John Muir, naturalist

Show me a guy who's afraid to look bad, and I'll show you a guy you can beat every time.

Lou Brock, baseball player

Play the game for more than you can afford to lose . . . Only then will you learn the game.

Sir Winston Churchill, British Prime Minister

I haven't failed; I just found 10,000 ways that don't work.

Thomas A. Edison, inventor

Nothing ventured, nothing gained.

American proverb

You reap what you sow.

Bible

You miss 100% of the shots you never take. I skate to where the puck is going to be, not to where it has been.

Wayne Gretzky, hockey player

If you're not failing every now and again, it's a sign you're not doing anything innovative.

Woody Allen, movie director

The man who insists upon seeing perfect clearness before he decides never decides.

Henri Frederic Amiel, poet

If you are scared to go to the brink, you are lost.

John Foster Dulles, U.S. Secretary of State

It's simply a matter of doing what you do best and not worrying about what the other fellow is going to do.

John Amos, actor and football player

All life is a chance. The person who goes farthest is the one who is willing to do and dare.

Dale Carnegie, success trainer and author

You've got to go out on a limb sometimes because that is where the fruit is.

Will Rogers, humorist and comedian

In order for you to profit from your mistakes, you have to go out and make some.

> Author unknown

And the day came when the risk to remain in a bud was more painful than the risk it took to blossom.

> Anais Nin, Cuban-French author

There's as much risk in doing nothing as in doing something.

> Trammell Crow, builder

A ship in port is safe, but that's not what ships are built for.

> Admiral Grace Murray Hopper, U.S. Navy

Success doesn't mean the absence of failures; it means the attainment of ultimate objectives. It means winning the war, not every battle.

> Edward C. Bliss, author

We cannot discover new oceans until we have the courage to lose sight of the shore.

> Muriel Chen, counselor

Never be afraid to try something new. Remember, amateurs built the ark; professionals built the titanic.

> Author unknown

Cautious, careful people, always casting about to preserve their reputations . . . can never effect a reform.

> Susan B. Anthony, woman's rights activist

I have failed over and over again in my life. And that's precisely why I succeed.

> Michael Jordan, basketball player

To try and fail is at least to learn. To fail to try is to suffer the loss of what might have been.

> Benjamin Franklin, statesman

Every great mistake has a halfway moment, a split second when it can be recalled and perhaps remedied.

Pearl Buck, writer

The successful man will profit from his mistakes and try again in a different way.

Dale Carnegie, success trainer and author

The man, who insists on seeing with perfect clearness before he decides, never decides.

Henri Frederic Amiel, Swiss philosopher and poet

Know How to Stay Motivated and Enthusiastic

The Success Focused Mind

Hard Work, Persistence and a Never-Die Attitude!

Overcoming Adversity and Getting out of a Sales Slump

Top Sales People Embrace Change and Prosper

Health is Wealth

Reward Yourself Regularly and Often

The Winning Sales Attitude and Mindset

Chapter 23

The Success Focused Mind

Eighty percent of success is showing up.
Woody Allen, movie director

The road to success is always under construction.
Author unknown

Try not to become a man of success but rather to become a man of value.
Elbert Einstein, scientist

My "Plan B" is better than anyone's "Plan A".
Michael Bloomberg, Mayor of New York City

Self trust is the first secret of success.
Ralph Waldo Emerson, philosopher

To laugh often and much; to win the respect of intelligent people and the affection of children; to earn the appreciation of honest critics and endure the betrayal of false friends; to appreciate beauty, to find the best in others; to leave the world a bit better, whether by a healthy child, a garden patch or a redeemed social condition; to know even one life has breathed easier because you have lived. This is to have succeeded.
Ralph Waldo Emerson, philosopher

The reward of a thing well done is to have done it.
Ralph Waldo Emerson, philosopher

What we call results are beginnings.
Ralph Waldo Emerson, philosopher

Success is something you have to put forth the effort for constantly; then maybe it'll come when you least expect it. Most people don't understand that.

Michael Jordan, six time NBA Finals MVP

Success requires a combination of discipline, optimism, humor, a willingness to share credit and good cigars and an ability to cut back-room deals.

Arnold Schwarzenegger, Governor of California, actor, athlete

For me life is continuously being hungry. The meaning of life is not simply to exist, to survive, but to move ahead, to go up, to achieve, to conquer.

Arnold Schwarzenegger, Governor of California, actor, athlete

I knew I was a winner back in the late sixties. I knew I was destined for great things. People will say that kind of thinking is totally immodest. I agree. Modesty is not a word that applies to me in any way—I hope it never will.

Arnold Schwarzenegger, Governor of California, actor, athlete

Start wide, expand further, and never look back.

Arnold Schwarzenegger, Governor of California, actor, athlete

Success is going from one failure to failure without losing your enthusiasm.

Sir Winston Churchill, British Prime Minister

When you do the common things in life in an uncommon way you will command the attention of the world.

George Washington Carver, scientist

Success is a journey, not a destination. The doing is often more important than the outcome.

Arthur Ashe, tennis player

Success is ninety-nine percent failure.

Soichiro Honda, founder of Honda

Many people dream of success. To me, success can only be achieved through repeated failure and introspection.

Soichiro Honda, founder of Honda

Success is how high you bounce when you hit bottom.

U.S. General George S. Patton

Success is simple. Do what is right, the right way, at the right time.

Arnold Glasow, author

A successful man is one who can lay a firm foundation with bricks that others throw at him.

David Brinkley, newscaster

Many of life's failures are people who did not realize how close they were to success when they gave up.

Thomas A. Edison, inventor

Success is your dreams with work clothes on.

Author unknown

Success is a journey, not a destination.

Nike Corporation Poster

We are what we repeatedly do. Excellence, then, is not an act, but a habit.

Aristotle, Greek philosopher

Successful and unsuccessful people do not vary greatly in their abilities. They vary in their desires to reach their potential.

John Maxwell, author and leadership expert

Success is not measured by what a man accomplishes, but by the opposition he has encountered and the courage with which he has maintained the struggle against overwhelming odds.

Charles Lindbergh, aviator

Don't measure yourself by what you have accomplished, but by what you should have accomplished with your ability.

John Wooden, basketball coach

Success is peace of mind in knowing you did your best.

John Wooden, basketball coach

The secret of success is consistency of purpose.

Benjamin Disraeli, Prime Minister of Great Britain

Listing your personal milestones is like storing a pocketful of sunshine for a rainy day.

Author unknown

Success is a journey, not a destination. The doing is often more important than the outcome.

Arthur Ashe, tennis player

The important thing to recognize is that it takes a team, and the team ought to get credit for the wins and the losses. Successes have many fathers, failures have none.

Philip Caldwell, automotive executive

Try not to become a man of success, but rather try to become a man of value.

Albert Einstein, scientist

The dictionary is the only place where success comes before work.

Mark Twain, American author

Success is that old ABC—ability, breaks and courage.

Charles Luckman, businessman

If you play to win, as I do, the game never ends.

Stan Mikita, hockey player

Men are born to succeed, not to fail.

Henry David Thoreau, writer and philosopher

Good, better, best; never let it rest till your good is better and your better is best.

Author unknown

By their fruits ye shall know them.
New Testament, Matthew 7:20

Back of every achievement is a proud wife and a surprised mother-in-law.
Brooks Hays, Attorney General of Arkansas

It is not going out of port, but the coming in that determines the success of a voyage.
Henry Ward Beecher, clergyman and abolitionist

He is rich or poor according to what he is, not according to what he has.
Henry Ward Beecher, clergyman and abolitionist

Success is more a function of consistent common sense than it is of genius.
An Wang, industrialist

Success doesn't come to you . . . you go to it.
Marva Collins, educator

Always bear in mind that your own resolution to succeed is more important than any other.
U.S President Abraham Lincoln

That some achieve great success, is proof to all that others can achieve it as well.
U.S. President Abraham Lincoln

Those who have succeeded at anything and don't mention luck are kidding themselves.
Larry King, TV and Radio Journalist

To do all that one is able to do is to be a man. To do all that one would like to do is to be a god.
Napoleon Bonaparte, French military and political leader

Success is the child of audacity.
Benjamin Disraeli, British Statesman

Success can make you go one of two ways. It can make you a Prima Donna—or it can smooth the edges, take away the insecurities, and let the nice things come out.

Barbara Walters, broadcaster

He is a wise man who does not grieve for the things that he has not, but rejoices for those that he has.

Epicurus, Greek philosopher

The secret to achieving wealth and success in your lifetime: Of your income, use 1/3rd to pay Uncle Sam, 1/3rd to live on, and 1/3rd to save and invest wisely.

Author unknown

Happiness is not a destination. It is a method of life.

Burton Hills, author

The best things in life aren't things.

Art Buchwald, columnist

Winning is the science of being totally prepared.

George Allen, football coach

Excellence is not an act, but a habit. The things you do the most are the things you will do the best.

Marva Collins, educator

The person who makes a success of living is the one who sees his goal steadily and aims for it unswervingly.

Cecil B. DeMille, Academy Award winning movie director

Success isn't permanent and failure isn't fatal.

Mike Ditka, football coach

You always pass failure on the way to success.

Mickey Rooney, actor

People seldom see the halting and painful steps by which the most insignificant success is achieved.

> Anne Sullivan, educator

Success is the sum of details.

> Harvey Firestone, industrialist

It is unhealthy to marinate in your own press clippings.

> Sam Walton, founder of Wal-Mart

Great success is built on failure, frustration, even catastrophe.

> Sumner Redstone, founder of Viacom

Success is mastering the circumstances you are in.

> Author unknown

Success is doing a thousand little things the right way—doing many of them over and over again.

> Charles Walgreen, drugstore titan

Success seems to be largely a matter of hanging on after others have let go.

> William Feather, publisher and author

Success is the sum of small efforts, repeated day in and day out.

> Robert Collier, self-help author

Three grand essentials to happiness in this life are something to do, somebody to love and something to hope for.

> Joseph Addison, English essayist and poet

Success doesn't come to you . . . you go to it.

> Marva Collins, educator

Success is not the result of spontaneous combustion. You must first set yourself on fire.

> Fred Shero, hockey player and coach

Success is not the key to happiness. Happiness is the key to success. If you love what you are doing, you will be successful.

Albert Schweitzer, theologian and philosopher

Success is getting what you want and happiness is wanting what you get.

Dale Carnegie, success trainer and author

People rarely succeed unless they have fun in what they are doing.

Dale Carnegie, success trainer and author

Success is never wondering what if?

Karrie Huffman

It takes 20 years to make an overnight success.

Eddie Cantor, comedian and actor

I have reached an age when, if someone tells me to wear socks, I don't have to.

Albert Einstein, scientist

The true measure of your worth includes all the benefits others have gained from your success.

Cullen Hightower, writer

The great value of life is to spend it on something that will outlast it.

James Truslow Adams, writer and historian

Where you end up isn't the most important thing. It's the road you take to get there. The road you take is what you'll look back on and call your life.

Tim Wiley

I wanted nothing else than to make the object as perfect as possible.

Erno Rubik, inventor

I firmly believe that any man's finest hour, his greatest fulfillment to all he holds dear, is the moment when he has worked his heart out in good cause and lies exhausted, but victorious, on the field of battle.

Vince Lombardi, football coach

There's only one way to succeed in anything and that is to give everything.

> Vince Lombardi, football coach

Success is following the pattern of life one most enjoys most.

> Al Capp, cartoonist

It is not how much we have, but how much we enjoy that makes us happy.

> Charles Spurgeon, clergyman

Whenever I hear "it can't be done," I know I'm close to success.

> Michael Flatley, dancer

How could there be any question of acquiring or possessing, when the one thing needful for a man is to become, to be at last, and die in the fullness of his being.

> Saint-Exupery

Helping someone is what life is all about.

> Willie Stargell, baseball player

A champion is afraid of losing. Everyone else is afraid of winning.

> Billie Jean King, tennis player

The toughest thing about success is that you've got to keep on being a success.

> Irving Berlin, songwriter

Don't aim at success; the more you aim at it and make it a target, the more you are going to miss it. For success, like happiness, cannot be pursued; it must ensue . . . as the unintended side effect of one's personal dedication to a course greater than oneself.

> Victor Frankl, from *Man's Search for Meaning*

Chapter 24

Hard work, persistence, and a Never Die Attitude!

You must pay the price if you wish to secure the blessings.
U.S. President Andrew Jackson

It is often the last key on the ring which opens the door.
Proverb

Fall seven times, stand up eight.
Japanese proverb

I hated every minute of training. But I said, "Don't quit. Train now and live the rest of my life as a champion."
Muhammad Ali, boxer

People who are unable to motivate themselves must be content with mediocrity, no matter how impressive their other talents.
Andrew Carnegie, steel magnate

The difference between "try" and "triumph" is just a little "umph"!
Bonnie Przybylski

Most people give up just when they're about to achieve success. They quit on the one yard line. They give up at the last minute of the game, one foot from a winning touchdown.
H. Ross Perot, billionaire

There is no substitute for hard work.
Thomas A. Edison, inventor

If there's a way to do it better, find it.
Thomas A. Edison, inventor

I have not failed 700 times. I have not failed once. I have succeeded in proving that those 700 ways will not work. When I have eliminated the ways that will not work, I will find the way that will work.

Thomas A. Edison, inventor

I have not failed. I've just found 10,000 ways that won't work.

Thomas A. Edison, inventor

Genius is one percent inspiration, ninety-nine percent perspiration.

Thomas A. Edison, inventor

A genius is a talented person who does his homework.

Thomas A. Edison, inventor

Everything comes to him who hustles while he waits.

Thomas A. Edison, inventor

The successful person makes a habit of doing what the failing person doesn't like to do.

Thomas A. Edison, inventor

If at first you don't succeed, welcome to the world that educated me.

Thomas A. Edison, inventor

With ordinary talent and extraordinary perseverance, all things are attainable.

Sir Thomas Buxton, British member of Parliament

If you are called to be a street sweeper, sweep streets even as Michelangelo painted or Beethoven composed music or Shakespeare wrote poetry. Sweep streets so well that all the hosts of heaven and earth will pause to say, "Here lived a great street sweeper who did his job well.

Martin Luther King, Jr., civil rights leader

To take the first step in faith, you don't have to see the whole staircase; just take the first step.

Martin Luther King, Jr., civil rights leader

To win takes a complete commitment of mind and body. When you can't make that commitment, they don't call you champion anymore.
Rocky Marciano, boxer

Little by little does the trick.
Aesop, Greek philosopher

Don't stay in bed, unless you can make money in bed.
George Burns, actor

Laziness travels so slowly that poverty soon overtakes it.
Benjamin Franklin, statesman

Up sluggard and waste not life. In the grave will be sleeping enough.
Benjamin Franklin, statesman

It is a rough road that leads to the heights of greatness.
Seneca, Roman philosopher

There is no traffic jams along the extra mile.
Roger Staubach, businessman and football player

Some men give up their designs when they have almost reached the goal. While others, on the contrary, obtain victory by exerting, at the last moment, more vigorous efforts than ever before.
Herodotus, Greek author

Nothing is really work unless you would rather be doing something else.
James Matthew Barrie, writer

Fall seven times; stand up eight.
Japanese proverb

God gives talent, work transforms talent into genius.
Anna Pavlova, ballerina

Chop your own wood and it will warm you twice.
Henry Ford, automotive titan

The only easy day was yesterday.
U.S. Navy SEALs slogan

No one is free who has not obtained the empire of himself.
Pythagoras, Greek philosopher

You may get skinned knees and elbows, but it's worth it if you score a spectacular goal.
Mia Hamm, Soccer player

The man who can drive himself further once the effort gets painful is the man who will win.
Roger Bannister, runner who broke the 4 minute mile

Effort only fully releases its reward after a person refuses to quit.
Napoleon Hill, from *Think and Grow Rich*

Effort only fully releases its reward after a person refuses to quit.
Napoleon Hill, from *Think and Grow Rich*

The majority of men meet with failure because of their lack of persistence in creating new plans to take the place of those which fail.
Napoleon Hill, from *Think and Grow Rich*

I find the harder I work, the more luck I seem to have.
U.S. President Thomas Jefferson

I'm a great believer in luck and I find the harder I work, the more I have of it.
U.S. President Thomas Jefferson

Success usually comes to those who are too busy to be looking for it.
Henry David Thoreau, writer and philosopher

If one advances confidently in the direction of his dreams and endeavors to live the life he had imagined, he will meet with a success unexpected in common hours.
Henry David Thoreau, writer and philosopher

There is no time for cut-and-dried monotony. There is time for work. And time for love. That leaves no other time.
Coco Chanel, fashion designer

The harder I work the luckier I get.
Alan "Ace" Greenberg, Wall Street Trader

If a business day is a social success, it has been a business failure.
Og Mandino, author

Whatever you do, do it with all your might. Work at it, early and late, in season and out of season, not leaving a stone unturned, and never deferring for a single hour that which can be done just as well now.
P.T. Barnum, circus founder

Luck is a dividend of sweat. The more you sweat, the luckier you get.
Ray Kroc, founder of McDonald's

Much effort, much prosperity.
Euripides, Greek playwright

Toil says the proverb is the sire of fame.
Euripides, Greek playwright

No great thing is created suddenly.
Epictetus, Greek philosopher

Nothing is beneath you if it is in the direction of your life.
Ralph Waldo Emerson, philosopher

He that rides his hobby gently must give way to him that rides his hobby hard.
Ralph Waldo Emerson, philosopher

That which we persist in doing becomes easier—not that the nature of the task has changed, but our ability to do has increased.
Ralph Waldo Emerson, philosopher

Our greatest glory is not in never failing, but in rising up every time we fall.
Ralph Waldo Emerson, philosopher

The line between failure and success is so fine that we scarcely know when we pass it; so fine that we often are on the line and do not know it.
>Ralph Waldo Emerson, philosopher

He who blames his tools is a poor carpenter.
>Confucius, Chinese philosopher

Choose a job you love and you will never have to work a day in your life.
>Confucius, Chinese philosopher

Trying is just a noisy way of not doing something.
>Author unknown

The words, "I'll try" is just vocalized failure.
>Chris Maloney

Luck is not chance. It's toil! Fortune's expensive smile is earned.
>Emily Dickinson, author

Nothing succeeds like excess.
>Oscar Wilde, Irish playwright and poet

I've had smarter people around me all my life, but I haven't run into one yet that can outwork me. And if they can't outwork you, then smarts aren't going to do them much good. That's just the way it is.
>Woody Hayes, football coach

You have to perform at a consistently higher level than others. That's the mark of a true professional. Professionalism has nothing to do with getting paid for your services.
>Joe Paterno, football coach

Go the extra mile that failures refuse to travel.
>Mary Kay Ash, cosmetic mogul

The key to success is simple: Do all the things that losers don't want to do!
>Kevin Dyerly, financial advisor

The loftiest towers rise from the ground.
> Chinese proverb

If the people knew how hard I work to gain mastery, it wouldn't seem wonderful at all.
> Michelangelo, Renaissance painter

Go and wake up your luck.
> Persian proverb

He that can work hard is born king of something.
> Thomas Carlyle, Scottish essayist and historian

Work spares us from three great evils: boredom, vice and need.
> Voltaire, French philosopher

The future has waited long enough. If we do not grasp it, other hands grasping hard and bloody will.
> Adlai Stevenson, diplomat and politician

Resolve never to quit, never give up, no matter what the situation.
> Jack Nicklaus, professional golfer

Trying is just a noisy way of not doing something.
> Author unknown

There is no gathering of the rose without being pricked by the thorns.
> From *Fables of Pilpay*

All hard work brings a profit, but mere talk leads only to poverty.
> Danish proverb

Work only half a day. It makes no difference which half—the first 12 hours or the last.
> Kemmons Wilson, founder of Holiday Inn

Effort is only effort when it begins to hurt.
> Vince Lombardi, football coach

The harder you work, the harder it is to surrender.
Vince Lombardi, football coach

The difference between a successful person and others is not a lack of strength, not a lack of knowledge, but rather a lack of will.
Vince Lombardi, football coach

Nothing can come of nothing.
William Shakespeare, English poet and playwright

Our doubts are traitors and make us lose the good we oft might win by fearing to attempt.
William Shakespeare, English poet and playwright

Behind every successful man there's a lot of unsuccessful years.
Everett M. Dirksen, U.S. Senator

Luck? I don't know anything about luck, I've never banked on it and I'm afraid of people who do. Luck to me is something else: hard work—and realizing what is opportunity and what isn't.
Lucille Ball, comedian and actress

Waiting for a great idea is a bad idea.
From the book, *Built to last*

God gives the milk, but not the pail.
British proverb

If you want to increase your success rate, double your failure rate.
Tom Watson, founder of IBM

The heights by great men reached and kept were not attained by sudden flight, but they while their companions slept, were toiling upward in the night.
Henry Wadsworth Longfellow, educator and poet

The first man gets the oyster; the second man gets the shell.
Andrew Carnegie, steel magnate

Ride lots!

Eddy Merckx, Five time winner of the Tour de France

Noise proves nothing. Often the hen who has merely laid an egg cackles as if she laid an asteroid.

Mark Twain, American author

Faith is believing what you know ain't so.

Mark Twain, American author

Nothing is easy to the unwilling.

Thomas Fuller, M.D.,

Don't believe the world owes you a living; the world owes you nothing—it was here first.

Unknown

They who lack talent expect things to happen without effort. They ascribe failure to a lack of education or inspiration or ability, or to misfortunes rather than to insufficient application. At the core of every true talent there is an awareness of the difficulties inherent in any achievement, and the confidence that by persistence and patience, something worthwhile will be realized. Thus talent is a species of vigor.

Eric Hoffer, philosopher and longshoreman

There are only two options regarding commitment. You're either "in" or you're "out." There's no such thing as life in between.

Pat Riley, basketball coach

The difference between a job and a career is the difference between 40 and 60 hours a week.

Robert Frost, poet

Iron rusts from disuse; stagnant water loses its purity and in cold weather becomes frozen; even so does inaction sap the vigor of the mind.

Leonardo da Vinci, inventor

The activist is not the man who says the river is dirty. The activist is the man who cleans up the river.

H. Ross Perot, billionaire

Unless you are willing to drench yourself in your work beyond the capacity of the average man, you are just not cut out for positions at the top.

J.C. Penny, retailer

The more I want to get something done, the less I call it work.

Richard Bach, writer and philosopher

Hard work spotlights the character of people: some turn up their sleeves, some turn up their noses and some don't turn up at all.

Sam Ewing, writer

Today I have given all that I can give. That which I have kept I have lost forever. Today I've given all—everything I had, my heart, blood and soul.

U.S. Marine slogan

Only those who risk going too far can possibly find out how far one can go.

T.S. Eliot, poet

What this power is I cannot say; all I know is that it exists and it becomes available only when a man is in that state of mind in which he knows exactly what he wants and is fully determined not to quit until he finds it.

Alexander Graham Bell, inventor

All hard work brings a profit, but mere talk leads only to poverty.

Proverbs 14:23

Don't believe the world owes you a living; the world owes you nothing—it was here first.

Robert Jones Burdette, clergyman and humorist

Do not pray for easy lives. Pray to be stronger men. Do not pray for tasks equal to your powers. Pray for powers equal to your tasks. Then the doing of your work shall be no miracle, but you shall be the miracle.

Phillips Brooks, clergyman

No one can arrive from being talented alone. God gives talent; work transforms talent into genius.

Anna Pavlova, dancer

Experience shows that success is due less to ability than to zeal.

Charles Buxton, author

You may be disappointed if you fail, but you are doomed if you don't try.

Beverly Sills, opera singer

The best parachute folders are those who jump themselves.

U.S. Army Ranger slogan

If the power to do hard work is not talent, it is the best possible substitute for it.

U. S. President James Garfield

It is better to die on your feet than live on your knees.

Ernest Hemingway, writer

No one would have crossed the ocean if he could have gotten off the ship in the storm.

Charles F. Kettering, inventor

Iron rusts from disuse; stagnant water loses its purity and in cold weather becomes frozen; even so does inaction sap the vigor of the mind.

Leonardo da Vinci, inventor

Sow your seed in the morning and at evening let your hands be idle, for you do not know which will succeed, whether this or that, or whether both will do equally well.

Ecclesiastes

It was on my fifth birthday that Papa put his hand on my shoulder and said, "Remember, my son, if you ever need a helping hand, you'll find one at the end of your arm."

Sam Levenson, comedian

Leisure time is the five or six hours when you sleep at night.

George Allen, football coach

People forget how fast you did a job, but they remember how well you did it.

Howard Newton, advertising executive

Work is man's most natural form of relaxation.

Dagobert Runes, Philosopher and author

Too much rest itself becomes a pain.

Homer, Greek poet

The lazy are always wanting to do something.

Marquis De Vauvenargues

Hard work spotlights the character of people: some turn up their sleeves, some turn up their noses, and some don't turn up at all.

Sam Ewig

You can't build a reputation on what you are going to do.

Henry Ford, automotive titan

Genius is seldom recognized for what it is: a great capacity for hard work.

Henry Ford, automotive titan

Nobody who ever gave his best regretted it.

George Halas, football coach

Hard work beats talent when talent doesn't work hard.

Tim Notke

I long to accomplish a great and noble task, but it is my chief duty to accomplish small tasks as if they were great and noble.

Helen Keller, author and activist

Nothing ever comes to one that is worth having except as a result of hard work.

Booker T. Washington, educator

Before the gates of excellence the high gods have placed sweat; long is the road thereto and rough and steep at first; but when the heights are reached, then there is ease, though grievously hard in the winning.

Hesiod, Greek poet

There are no short cuts to any place worth going.

Author unknown

Efficiency is intelligent laziness.

David Dunham

Show me a man who cannot bother to do little things and I'll show you a man who cannot be trusted to do big things.

Lawrence Bell, aviation businessman

Luck is not chance, it's toil. Fortune's expensive smile is earned.

Emily Dickinson, writer and poet

If people knew how hard I worked to get my mastery, it wouldn't seem so wonderful after all.

Michelangelo, artist

Honor lies in honest toil.

U. S. President Grover Cleveland

A career is not made up of a success in front of that audience that night.

Isaac Stern, violinist

What counts is not necessarily the size of the dog in the fight—it's the size of the fight in the dog.
> U.S. President Dwight D. Eisenhower

Without struggle there is no progress.
> Frederick Douglass, slavery abolitionist

I couldn't wait for success, so I went along without it.
> Jonathan Winters, actor

We must all suffer from one of two pains: the pain of discipline or the pain of regret. The difference is discipline weighs ounces while regret weighs tons.
> Jim Rohn, motivational coach

The highest reward for a person's toil is not what they get for it, but what they become by it.
> John Ruskin, critic

Aerodynamically, the bee shouldn't be able to fly, but the bumblebee doesn't know it so it goes on flying anyway.
> Mary Kay Ash, cosmetic mogul

Work spares us from three great evils: boredom, vice and need.
> Voltaire, French philosopher

You can't get much done in life if you only work on the days your feel good.
> Jerry West, Los Angeles Lakers

Persistent people begin their success where others end in failure.
> Edward Eggleston, writer

Most people never run far enough on their first wind to find out they've got a second.
> William James, philosopher

I never quit trying; I never felt that I didn't have a chance to win.
> Arnold Palmer, professional golfer

Always bear in mind that your own resolution to succeed is more important than any one thing.
U.S. President Abraham Lincoln

Chance never helps those who do not help themselves
Sophocles, Greek playwright

I've had smarter people around me all my life, but I haven't run into one yet that can outwork me. And if they can't outwork you, then smarts aren't going to do them much good.
Woody Hayes, college football coach

Do your homework!
Mom

An idea is a curious thing. It will not work unless you do.
Hannah Whitall Smith, religious leader

Success is dependent upon the glands—the sweat glands.
Zig Ziglar, sales trainer

Timid salespeople have skinny children.
Zig Ziglar, sales trainer

Do a little more each day than you think you possibly can.
Lowell Thomas, writer

How long should you try? Until.
Jim Rohn, motivational coach

Hard work is the key to success. There's a price to pay for everything. Are you prepared to pay it?
Tiger Woods, golfer

Nothing will work unless you do.
Maya Angelou, writer and poet

Life shrinks or expands in proportion to one's courage.
Anais Nin, Cuban-French author

Do not go gentle into that good night.

> Dylan Thomas, writer

People of mediocre ability sometimes achieve outstanding success because they don't know when to quit. Most people succeed because they are determined to.

> George Allen, football coach

A Champion is someone who gets up when he can't.

> Jack Dempsey, Boxer

By perseverance the snail reached the ark.

> Charles Spurgeon, author

Press on. Nothing in the world can take the place of persistence. Talent will not; nothing is more common than unsuccessful men with talent. Genius will not; unrewarded genius is almost a proverb. Education alone will not; the world is full of educated derelicts. Persistence and determination alone are omnipotent.

> U.S. President Calvin Coolidge

A small daily task, if it be really daily, will beat the labors of a spasmodic Hercules.

> Anthony Trollope, English novelist

This one thing I do . . . I press toward the mark.

> St. Paul the Apostle

Victory: a matter of staying power.

> Elbert Hubbard, writer

The first time you quit, it's hard. The second time, it gets easier. The third time, you don't even have to think about it.

> Bear Bryant, football coach

Victory belongs to the most persevering.

> Napoleon Bonaparte, French military and political leader

Ultimately, winning and success comes down to personal resolve.
U.S. Navy Seal Instructor

Just when the caterpillar thought its world was over . . . it changed into a butterfly.
Zen saying

Only one who devotes himself to a cause with his whole strength and soul can be a true master. For this reason mastery demands all of a person.
Albert Einstein, physicist

Great people are just ordinary people with an extraordinary amount of determination.
Garner Dunkerley, Sr., businessman

This is a Timex World—you're gonna take a licking, but you gotta keep on ticking!
Ernesto Quinonez, author

Many strokes overthrow the tallest oaks.
John Lyly, English poet

Success is the result of hard work, learning from failure, loyalty and persistence.
U.S. General Colin Powell

It takes guts to get into the ring, but it takes a lot of heart to remain in it.
Unknown

When I thought I couldn't go on, I forced myself to keep going. My success is based on persistence, not luck.
Estee Lauder, cosmetic entrepreneur

To endure what is unendurable is true endurance.
Japanese proverb

To bear is to conquer our fate.
Thomas Campbell, Scottish poet

We may be masters of our every lot—by bearing it.
>Virgil, Roman poet

Finish out the game Sport!
>Gordon Gecko, in the movie *Wall Street*

Courage is fear holding on a minute longer.
>U.S. General George S. Patton

In business, sometimes prospects may seem darkest when really they are on the turn. A little more persistence, a little more effort, and what seemed hopeless failure may turn to glorious success.
>E Hubbard, writer

It isn't hard to be good from time to time ... what's tough is being good every day.
>Willie Mays, Hall of Fame Baseball player

A professional is an amateur who didn't quit.
>Richard Bach, writer

Success seems to be largely a matter of hanging on after others have let go.
>William Feather, publisher and author

Persistence—not perfection.
>Bill Phillips, health and fitness expert

There can be no progress if people have no faith in tomorrow.
>U.S. President John F. Kennedy

Persistence: 1. to continue steadily, especially in spite of opposition. Synonym: Persevering, steadfast, resolute. See Stubborn.
>Dictionary definition

He conquers who endures.
>Persius, Roman poet

Don't let the bastards grind you down.
>U.S. General Joseph Stilwell

No person was ever honored for what he received. Honor has been the reward for what he gave.
U.S. President Calvin Coolidge

Do not let what you cannot do interfere with what you can do.
John Wooden, basketball coach

According to aerodynamic laws, the bumblebee cannot fly. Its body weight is not the right proportion to its wingspan. Ignoring these laws, the bee flies anyway.
M. Sainte-Lague, French mathematician and writer

Mighty rivers can easily be leaped at their source.
Publilius Syrus, Roman philosopher

Do not despise the bottom rungs in the ascent to greatness.
Publilius Syrus, Roman philosopher

I realized early on that success was tied to not giving up. Most people in this business gave up and went on to other things. If you simply didn't give up, you would outlast the people who came in on the bus with you.
Harrison Ford, actor

To be somebody, you must last.
Ruth Gordon, actress

To me, success can be achieved only through repeated failure and introspection. In fact, success represents the one percent of your work that results from the 99% that is called failure.
Soichiro Honda, industrialist

All that stands between you and the top of the ladder is the ladder.
Author Unknown

If you want to increase your success rate, double your failure rate.
Thomas Watson Sr., founder of IBM

A professional writer is an amateur who didn't quit.
Richard Bach, writer

You get the best out of others when you give the best of yourself.

Harry Firestone, tire mogul

It's always too early to quit!

Dr. Norman Vincent Peale, spiritual leader

Always bear in mind that your own resolution to succeed is more important than any one thing.

U.S. President Abraham Lincoln

Have patience with all things, but chiefly have patience with yourself. Do not lose courage in considering your own imperfections but instantly set about remedying them—every day begin the task anew.

St. Francis de Sales, clergyman

You've got to get up every morning with determination if you're going to go to bed with satisfaction.

George Horace Lorimer, editor of *The Saturday Evening Post*

Where most of us end up there is no knowing, but the hell-bent get where they are going.

James Thurber, cartoonist

It is not the mountain we conquer, but ourselves.

Sir Edmund Hillary, first to summit Mt. Everest

A minute's success pays the failure of years.

Robert Browning, poet

Character consists of what you do on the third and fourth tries.

James Michener, author

Courage is the thing. All goes if courage goes.

J.M. Barrie, Scottish novelist

None but the brave deserves the fair.

John Dryden, English poet

I do not think that there is any other quality so essential to success of any kind as the quality of perseverance. It overcomes almost everything, even nature.

John D. Rockefeller, oil mogul

Faith is to believe what you do not yet see; the reward for this faith is to see what you believe.

St. Augustine

What is faith but a kind of betting or a speculation after all.

Samuel Butler, novelist

You can do very little faith, but you can do nothing without it.

Samuel Butler, novelist

Faith is the pier less bridge supporting what we see unto the scene that we do not.

Emily Dickinson, author

Not truth, but faith it is that keeps the world alive.

Edna St. Vincent Mallay, poet and playwright

It is your own assent to yourself and the constant voice of your own reason and not of others that should make you believe.

Pascal, French mathematician and philosopher

Whenever you see a successful business, someone once made a courageous decision.

Peter F. Drucker, business writer and strategist

I have no exception of making a hit every time I come to bat. What I seek is the highest possible batting average.

U.S. President Franklin D. Roosevelt

Become so wrapped up in something that you forget to be afraid.

Lady Bird Johnson, First Lady

One worthwhile task carried to a successful conclusion is worth half-a-hundred half-finished tasks.

Malcolm S. Forbes, publisher

Patience is never more important than when you are at the edge of losing it.

O.A. Battista, chemist

Be ashamed to die until you have won some victory for humanity.

Horace Mann, education reformer

Always remember that striving and struggle precede success, even in the dictionary.

Sarah Ban Breathnach, writer

Let me tell you the secret that has led me to my goal. My strength lies solely in my tenacity.

Louis Pasteur, chemist and scientist

Ambition can creep as well as soar.

Edmund Burke, politician

Most of the important things in the world have been accomplished by people who have kept on trying when there seemed to be no hope at all.

Dale Carnegie, success trainer and author

Champions keep playing until they get it right.

Billy Jean King, tennis superstar

God grants victory to perseverance.

Simon Bolivar, Spanish colonist and leader

The past of least resistance is the path of the loser.

H.G. Wells, author

Every winner has scars.

Herbert Casson, journalist

A man is not finished when he is defeated. He is finished when he quits.

U.S. President Richard Nixon

Sweat plus sacrifice equals success.

Charley Finley, professional baseball team owner

The man who makes it the habit of his life to go to bed at 9 o'clock usually gets rich and is always reliable. Of course, going to bed does not make him rich. I merely mean that such a man will in all probability be up early in the morning and do a big day's work, so his weary bines put him to bed early. It's all a matter of habit, and good habits in America make a man rich. Rich is a result of habit.

John Jacob Astor

When you feel how depressingly, slowly you climb; it's well to remember that Things Take Time.

Piet Hein, Danish scientist and inventor

One person with a commitment is worth more than 100 people who have only an interest.

Mary Crowley, writer

Never give up, for that is just the place and time that the tide will turn.

Harriet Beecher Stowe, writer

Satisfaction does not come with achievement, but with effort. Full effort is full victory.

Mahatma Gandhi, spiritual and political leader of India

A professional is someone who can do his best work when he doesn't feel like it.

Alistair Cooke, journalist

What the country needs is dirtier fingernails and cleaner minds.

Will Rogers, comedian and humorist

Many of life's failures are people who did not realize how close they were to success when they gave up.

Thomas A. Edison, inventor

If you are going through hell—keep going!

> Sir Winston Churchill, British Prime Minister

The ability to work hard is, in itself a talent.

> Sir Winston Churchill, British Prime Minister

It is not enough that we do our best; sometimes we have to do what's required.

> Sir Winston Churchill, British Prime Minister

Never give in! Never give in! Never, never, never—in nothing great or small, large or petty. Never give in, except to convictions of honour and good sense.

> Sir Winston Churchill, British Prime Minister

Luck favors the persistent.

> Sir Winston Churchill, British Prime Minister

Sometimes our best is simply not enough, we have to do what is required.

> Sir Winston Churchill, British Prime Minister

Never, never, never give up!

> Sir Winston Churchill, British Prime Minister

The big shots are only the little shots who keep shooting.

> Christopher Morley, journalist and novelist

You may have to fight a battle more than once to win it.

> Margaret Thatcher, British Prime Minister

Chapter 25

Overcoming Adversity and
Getting Out of a Sales Slump

How much would they pay the matador if the bull didn't have any horns?

Spanish saying

When everything seems to be going against you, remember that the airplane takes off against the wind, not with it.

Henry Ford, automotive titan

The first rule of holes: When you're in one, stop digging.

Molly Ivins, author and columnist

Turn the page.

Aldo Gucci, founder of Gucci

We have to act our way into a new way of thinking rather than think our way into a new way of acting.

Ralph Waldo Emerson, philosopher

Your own mind is a sacred enclosure into which nothing harmful can enter except by your permission.

Ralph Waldo Emerson, philosopher

The great man is not convulsible or tormentable; events pass over him without much impression.

Ralph Waldo Emerson, philosopher

The wise man in the storm prays to God, not for safety from the danger, but for deliverance from fear.

Ralph Waldo Emerson, philosopher

One day, good or bad, does not make a week. One week does not make a month. One month does not make a year. One year does not make a career.

Andrew Niccoletta, Wall Streeter

My motto was always to keep swinging. Whether I was in a slump or feeling badly or having trouble off the field, the only thing to do was keep swinging.

Hank Aaron, homerun hitter

Adversity causes some men to break; others to break records.

William Ward, author

Kites rise highest against the wind—not with it.

Sir Winston Churchill, British Prime Minister

When you're going through hell, keep going.

Sir Winston Churchill, British Prime Minister

When I look back on all my worries, I remember the story of the old man who said on his deathbed that he had a lot of trouble in his life, most of which had never happened.

Sir Winston Churchill, British Prime Minister

You will never do anything in this world without courage. It is the greatest quality of the mind next to honour.

Aristotle, Greek philosopher

The measure of a man is the way he bears up under misfortune.

Plutarch, Greek author

Concern should drive us into action and not into a depression. No man is free who cannot control himself.

Pythagoras, Greek philosopher

He that wrestles with us strengthens our nerves and sharpens our skill. Our antagonist is our helper.

Edmund Burke, Irish politician and philosopher

Difficulties are just things to overcome, after all.

> Ernest Shackleton, world explorer

The ultimate measure of a man is not where he stands in moments of comfort and convenience, but where he stands at times of challenge and controversy.

> Martin Luther king, Jr., civil rights leader

There is nothing to fear but fear itself.

> U.S. President Franklin D. Roosevelt

It is better to light one small candle than to curse the darkness.

> Confucius, Chinese philosopher

When you get to the end of your rope, tie a knot and hang on!

> U.S. President Franklin D. Roosevelt

Women are like teabags. We don't know our true strength until we are in hot water!

> Eleanor Roosevelt, First Lady

Adversity brings out our hidden potential.

> Jeff Keller, motivational speaker and writer

Don't let yesterday use up too much of today.

> Cherokee proverb

People are always blaming their circumstances for what they are. I do not believe in circumstances. The people who get on in this world are the people who get up and look for the circumstances they want, and if they cannot find them, make them.

> George Bernard Shaw, author

Problems are messages.

> Shakti Gawain, motivational writer

I've never been poor, only broke. Being poor is a frame of mind. Being broke is only a temporary situation.

> Mike Todd, movie producer

Necessity is the mother of invention.
> Plato, Greek philosopher

Do not let what you cannot do interfere with what you can do.
> John Wooden, basketball coach

Fear is my only carriage so I got to push on through. Everything's gonna be alright.
> Bob Marley, Reggae musician

Pressure is your best friend. It helps you focus on your job, rise earlier, stay later and creates your passion.
> Rick Pitino, basketball coach

The basic difference between an ordinary man and a warrior is that a warrior takes everything as a challenge, while an ordinary man takes everything either as a blessing or a curse.
> From Tales of Power, Carlos Castaneda

As wise women and men in every culture tell us; the art of life is not controlling what happens to us, but using what happens to us.
> Gloria Steinem, author and activist

The best way to escape from a problem is to solve it.
> Alan Saporta, author

We are continually faced by great opportunities brilliantly disguised as insoluble problems.
> Lee Iacocca, automotive executive

What doesn't kill us makes us stronger.
> Friedrich Nietzsche, German philosopher

He who has a "why" to live can bear with almost any "how".
> Friedrich Nietzsche, German philosopher

Ones best success comes after their greatest disappointment.
> Henry Ward Beecher, clergyman and abolitionist

A smooth sea never made a skilled mariner.
An old English proverb

No one would have crossed the ocean if he could have gotten off the ship in the storm.
Charles Kettering, inventor

Success is how high you bounce when you hit bottom.
U.S. General George S. Patton

Nobody talks of entrepreneurship as survival, but that's exactly what it is and what nurtures creative thinking.
Anita Roddick, founder of The Body Shop

Obstacles cannot crush me. Every obstacle yields to stern resolve. He who is fixed to a star does not change his mind.
Leonardo Da Vinci, inventor

Sweet is pleasure after pain.
John Dryden. English poet

Tough times don't build character, tough times reveals character.
Author unknown

Travel, trouble, music, art, a kiss, a frock, a rhyme I never said they feed my heart, but still they pass my time.
Dorothy Parker, writer and poet

Whenever you see darkness, there is extraordinary opportunity for the light to burn brighter.
Bono, musician

I love the man who can smile in trouble, who can gather strength from distress and grow brave by reflection.
Thomas Paine, revolutionary and writer

When one door closes, another door opens; but we so often look so long and so regretfully upon the closed door that we do not see the ones which open for us.

Alexander Graham Bell, inventor

A little uncertainty is good for everything.

Henry Kissinger, U.S. Secretary of State

Don't worry about the world coming to an end today; it's already tomorrow in Australia.

Charles Schultz, cartoonist

Even after a bad harvest, there must be sowing.

Seneca, Roman philosopher

A man that suffers before it is necessary suffers more than necessary.

Seneca, Roman philosopher

It is a rough road that leads to the heights of greatness.

Seneca, Roman philosopher

If we had no winter, the spring would not be so pleasant. If we did not sometimes taste of adversity, prosperity would not be so welcome.

Anna Bradstreet, poet

It's a good thing to have all the props pulled out from under us occasionally. It gives us some sense of what is rock under our feet and what is sand.

Madeline L' Engle, writer

Troubles, like babies, grow larger by nursing.

Lady Holland, 19th Century English socialite

We have more ability than willpower and it's often an excuse to ourselves that we imagine that things are impossible.

La Rochefoucauld, French author

You may have a fresh start any moment you choose, for this thing we call a "failure" is not in falling down, but in staying down.

Mark Pickford, actress

He who fears he shall suffer already suffers what he fears.

Montaigne, French Renaissance writer

A smooth sea never made a skilled mariner.

English proverb

If you want the rainbow . . . you've got to put up with the rain.

Jimmy Durante, singer

A man's doubts and fears are his worst enemies.

William Wrigley Jr., chewing gum executive

What was was! What is is!

Sparky Anderson, baseball coach

Never confuse a single defeat with a final defeat.

F. Scott Fitzgerald, author

Vitality shows not only in the ability to persist, but in the ability to start over.

F. Scott Fitzgerald, author

Every adversity has the seed of an equivalent or greater benefit.

Napoleon Hill, from *Think and Grow Rich*

Turn that frown upside down.

Richard Simmons, fitness personality

It's alright. It's ok. We still love you anyway!

A popular cheerleading cheer

Nothing has happened to you unless you make much of it.

Menander, Greek playwright

Hells Bells, when times are bad is when you want to build. Why wait for things to pick up so everything will cost you more. If a location is good enough to buy, we want to build on it right away and be in there before the competition.

Ray Kroc, founder of McDonalds

Although the world is full of suffering, it is also full of overcoming it.

Helen Keller, author and activist

One can never consent to creep when one feels an impulse to soar.

Helen Keller, author and activist

Failure is good. It's fertilizer. Everything I've learned about coaching I've learned from making mistakes.

Rick Pitino, basketball coach

All that is necessary to break the spell of inertia and frustration is this: Act as if it were impossible to fail.

Dorothea Brande, writer

It is part of the American character to consider nothing as desperate.

U.S. President Thomas Jefferson

Success isn't permanent and failure isn't fatal.

Mike Ditka, football coach

To a brave man, good and bad luck are like his right and left hand. He uses both.

St. Catherine of Siena

The ultimate measure of a man is not where he stands in moments of comfort, but where he stands in times of challenge and controversy.

Martin Luther King, Jr., civil rights leader

Deep faith eliminates fear.

Lech Walesa, President of Poland

A bold heart is half the battle.
> U.S. President Dwight Eisenhower

The only way out of a problem is through it.
> Myrna Radl, psychologist

Virtually nothing comes out right the first time. Failures, repeated failures, are finger posts on the road to achievement. The only time you don't fail is the last time you try something and it works. One fails forward toward success.
> Charles Kettering, inventor

People and rubber bands have one thing in common: they must be stretched to be effective.
> John Maxwell, writer

When you're sick and tired of being sick and tired, you'll stop being sick and tired.
> Author unknown

When things are steep, remember to be level-headed.
> U.S. President Theodore Roosevelt

Adversity is another way to measure the greatness of individuals. I never had a crisis that didn't make me stronger.
> Lou Holtz, football coach

I walk firmer and more secure up hill than down.
> Michel de Montaigne, writer

Never think that you're not good enough yourself. A man should never think that. People will take you very much at your own reckoning.
> Anthony Trollope, novelist

Sweet are the uses of adversity, which like the toad, ugly and venomous, wears yet a precious jewel in his head.
> William Shakespeare, English playwright

The heart prefers to move against the grain of circumstance; perversity is the soul's very life.
John Updike, writer

A winner is big enough to admit his mistakes, smart enough to profit from them and strong enough to correct them.
John Maxwell, author

Don't defy the diagnosis, try to defy the verdict.
Norman Cousins, writer

I would never have amounted to anything were it not for adversity. I was forced to come up the hard way.
J.C. Penny, retailer

The best way out is always through.
Robert Frost, poet

Every exit is an entry somewhere.
Tom Stoppard, playwright

You can discover what your enemy fears most by observing the means he uses to frighten you.
Eric Hoffer, philosopher and longshoreman

Carry the battle to them. Don't let them bring it to you. Put them on the defensive.
U.S. President Harry S. Truman

Do not pray for tasks equal to your powers, pray for powers equal to your tasks.
Phillips Brooks, bishop

God's delays are not God's denials.
Dr. Robert Schuller, spiritual leader

The good news is that the bad news can be turned into good news when you change your attitude.
Dr. Robert Schuler, spiritual leader

Empty pockets never held anyone back. Only empty heads and empty hearts can do that.

Dr. Norman Vincent Peale, author and spiritual leader

Positive thinking is a form of thought which habitually looks for the best results from the worst conditions.

Dr. Norman Vincent Peale, author and spiritual leader

In a philosophical dispute, he gains most who is defeated, since he learns most.

Epicurus, philosopher

To tremble before anticipated evils is to bemoan what thou has never lost.

Johann Wolfgang von Goethe, German poet

Inside the ring or out, ain't nothing wrong with going down. It's staying down that's wrong.

Muhammad Ali, boxer

Defeat never comes to any man until he admits it.

Josephus Daniels, politician and publisher

But man is not made for defeat. A man can be destroyed but not defeated.

Ernest Hemingway, writer

Defeat is not the worst of failures. Not to have tried is the true failure.

George E. Woodberry, critic and poet

Prosperity is a great teacher; adversity a greater.

William Hazlitt, English writer

Failure is success if we learned from it.

Malcolm Forbes, publisher

There is no security on this earth, there is only opportunity.

U.S. General Douglas MacArthur

We are not retreating; we are advancing in another direction.
U.S. General Douglas MacArthur

Courage and perseverance have a magical talisman, before which difficulties disappear and obstacles vanish into air.
U.S. President John Quincy Adams

In difficult situations when hope seems feeble, the boldest plans are the safest.
Livy, Roman historian

The best mask for demoralization is daring.
Lucan, Roman poet

The word "crisis" in Chinese is composed of two characters: the first, the symbol of danger; the second, opportunity.
U.S. President John F. Kennedy

Great crisis produce great men and great deeds of courage.
U.S. President John F. Kennedy

Every area of trouble gives out a ray of hope; and the one unchangeable certainty is that nothing is certain or unchangeable.
U.S. President John F. Kennedy

Facing it, always facing it, that's the way to get through. Face it.
Joseph Conrad, English novelist

If winter comes, can spring be far behind.
Percy Bysshe Shelley, English poet

In times like these, it helps to recall that there have always been times like these.
Paul Harvey, radio personality

Do just once what others say you can't do and you will never pay attention to their limitations again.
James Cook, explorer

I wish it, I command it! Let my will take the place of reason.
> Juvenal, Roman poet

If you want to lift yourself up, lift someone else up.
> Booker T. Washington, educator

I've always felt it was not up to anyone else to make me give my best.
> Hakeem Olajuwon, basketball player

Believe that your life is worth living and your belief will create the fact.
> William James, psychologist and philosopher

Ninety percent of this game is half mental.
> Yogi Berra, baseball player and coach

It's never too late to be who you might have been.
> George Elliot, English novelist

Motivation is everything. You can do the work of two people, but you can't be two people. Instead, you have to inspire the next guy down the line and get him to inspire his people.
> Lee Iacocca, automotive executive

If you don't believe in yourself, how can you ask others to?
> Author unknown

Never for the sake of peace and quiet deny your own experience or convictions.
> Dag Hammarskjold, statesmen

Thicken your skin if you want to win.
> Steve Poltz, musician

The difference between a rut and a grave is the depth.
> Gerald Burrill, clergyman

I am not discouraged, because every wrong attempt discarded is another step forward.

Thomas A. Edison, inventor

Slumps are like a soft bed. They're easy to get into and hard to get out of.

Johnny Bench, baseball player

Patience is bitter, but its reward is sweet.

Author unknown

We would accomplish many more things if we did not think of them as impossible.

Vince Lombardi, football coach

In the middle of difficulty lies opportunity.

Albert Einstein, scientist

We cannot solve our problems with the same thinking we used when we recreated them.

Albert Einstein, scientist

Keep in mind that neither success nor failure is ever final.

Roger Babson, founder of *Babson College*

Follow the first law of holes: if you are in one, stop digging.

Lord Denis Healy, British Statesman

Not everything that is faced can be changed, but nothing can be changed until it is faced.

James Baldwin, author

The meaning I picked, the one that changed my life: Overcome fear, behold wonder.

Aeschylus, Greek playwright

Fear is static that prevents me from hearing my intuition.

Hugh Prather, author and clergyman

There is no abiding success without commitment.
Anthony Robbins success trainer and author

Some people freeze to death in the winter; other people ski!
Anthony Robbins, success trainer and author

Worry does not empty tomorrow of its sorrow; it empties today of its strength.
Corrie Ten Boom, author and Holocaust survivor

Keep faith in all beautiful things; in the sun when it is hidden, in the spring when it is gone.
Roy Gilson, author

Miracles start to happen when you give as much energy to your dreams as you do to your fears.
Richard Wilkins, musician and performer

I have been through some terrible things in my life, some of which actually happened.
Mark Twain, American author

Ones best successes comes after their greatest disappointments.
Henry Ward Beecher, clergyman and abolitionist

The season of failure is the best time for sowing the seeds of success.
Paramahansa Yogananda, Indian yogi and guru

If life gives us rocks, it's our choice whether to build a bridge or a wall.
Author unknown

The closest you will ever come in this life to an orderly universe is a good library.
Ashleigh Brilliant, cartoonist

Worry is like a rocking chair—it gives you something to do, but it doesn't get you anywhere.
Dorothy Galyean, author

Obstacles don't have to stop you. If you run into a wall, don't turn around and give up. Figure out how to climb it, go through it, or work around it.

Michael Jordan, basketball player

People are always blaming their circumstances for what they are. I do not believe in circumstances. The people who get on in this world are the people who get up and look for the circumstances they want, and if they cannot find them, make them.

George Bernard Shaw, author

Let us be of good cheer, remembering that the misfortunes hardest to bear are those that never come.

James Russell Lowell, poet

I merely took the energy it takes to pout and wrote some blues.

Duke Ellington, jazz musician

If you tell every step, you will make a long journey of it.

Thomas Fuller, M.D.

To act coolly, intelligently and prudently in perilous circumstances is the test of a man and also a nation.

Adlai Stevenson, politician and diplomat

It's not the situation; it's your reaction to the situation.

Bob Conklin, motivational and success trainer

The greater the obstacle, the more glory in overcoming it.

Moliere, French poet and playwright

Chapter 26

Top Sales People Embrace Change and Prosper

It is not the strongest of the species that survive, nor the most intelligent, but the one most responsive to change.
Charles Darwin, scientist

Change before you have to.
Jack Welch, CEO of General Electric

Change is the law of life. And those who look only to the past or the present are certain to miss the future.
U.S. President John F. Kennedy

Every exit is an entry somewhere.
Tom Stoppard, English playwright

Things do not change; we change.
Henry David Thoreau, philosopher

Without change, something sleeps inside us, and seldom awakens. The sleeper must awaken.
Frank Herbert, science fiction writer

One must change one's tactics every 10 years if one wishes to maintain one's superiority.
Napoleon Bonaparte, French military and political leader

A great wind of change is blowing and that gives you either imagination or a headache.
Catherine the Great, Empress of Russia

There is always a disposition in people's minds to think that existing conditions will be permanent. When the market is down and dull, it is hard to make people believe that this is the prelude to a period of activity and advance. When prices are up and the country is prosperous, it is always said that while preceding booms have not lasted, there are circumstances connected with this one which will make it unlike its predecessors and give assurance of permanency. The one fact pertaining to all conditions is that they will change.

> Charles H. Dow, co-founder of Dow Jones & Company

Nothing is permanent but change.

> Heraclitus, philosopher

Change alone is eternal, perpetual, immortal.

> Arthur Schopenhauer, German philosopher

The displacement of a little sand can change occasionally the course of deep rivers.

> Manuel Gonzalez Prada, Peruvian politician

The more things change, the more they remain the same.

> Alphonse Karr, French author

He who rejects change is the architect of decay. The only human institution which rejects progress is the cemetery.

> Harold Wilson, British Prime Minister

Change really becomes a necessity when we try not to do it.

> Anne Wilson Schaef, writer and lecturer

Our dilemma is that we hate change and love it at the same time; what we really want is for things to remain the same but get better.

> Sydney J. Harris, journalist

The only certainty is that nothing is certain.

> Pliny the Elder, philosopher

Softness triumphs over hardness, feebleness over strength. What is malleable is always superior to that which is immovable. This is the principle of controlling things by going along with them, of mastery through adaptation.

Lao Tzu, Father of Taoism

We live in a moment of history where change is so speeded up that we begin to see the present only when it is already disappearing.

R. D. Lang, writer

A thought is an idea in transit.

Pythagoras, Greek philosopher

Only the wisest and stupidest of men never change.

Confucius, Chinese philosopher

It is not necessary to change. Survival is not mandatory.

W. Edwards Deming

You must be the change you wish to see in the world.

Mahatma Gandhi, spiritual and political leader of India

As human beings, our greatness lies not so much in being able to remake the world . . . as in being able to remake ourselves.

Mahatma Gandhi, spiritual and political leader of India

A competitive world has two possibilities for you: you can lose or, of you want to win, you can change.

Lester C. Thurow, Dean of MIT Sloan School of Management

If we don't change, we don' grow. If we don't grow, we aren't really living.

Gail Sheehy, writer

We must always change, renew and rejuvenate ourselves—otherwise we harden.

Johann Wolfgang von Goethe, German poet and writer

If you're in a bad situation, don't worry it'll change. If you're in a good situation, don't worry it'll change.

John A. Simone, Sr., author

The most effective way to manage change is to create it.

Peter Drucker, business author

The world hates change, yet it is the only thing that has brought progress.

Charles Kettering, scientist

To dispose a soul to action we must upset its equilibrium.

Eric Hoffer, longshoreman and philosopher

To keep ahead, each of us, no matter what our task, must search for new and better methods, for even that which we now do well must be done even better tomorrow.

James Franklin Bell, U.S. Army

The real voyage of discovery consists not in seeking new landscapes, but in seeing with new eyes.

Marcel Proust, French novelist

We all have big changes in our lives that are more or less a second chance.

Harrison Ford, actor

Just because everything is different doesn't mean anything has changed.

Irene Peter, author

Chapter 27

Health is Wealth

The first wealth is health.
Ralph Waldo Emerson, philosopher

The health of the eye seems to demand a horizon. We are never tired, so long as we can see far enough.
Ralph Waldo Emerson, philosopher

Health is the first muse, and sleep is the condition to produce it.
Ralph Waldo Emerson, philosopher

The greatest wealth is health.
Virgil, Roman poet

The best activities for your health are pumping and humping.
Arnold Schwarzenegger, Governor of California, actor, athlete

All truly great thoughts are conceived while walking.
Friedrich Nietzsche, German philosopher

Lack of activity destroys the good condition of every human being, while movement and methodical physical exercise save it and preserve it.
Plato, Greek philosopher

Those who think they have not time for bodily exercise will sooner or later have to find time for illness.
Edward Stanley, British statesman

The health of nations is more important than the wealth of nations.
Will Durant, philosopher

I say exercise is equivalent to a dose of Ritalin, a little Adderal and a little bit of Prozac.

Dr. John Ratey, psychiatrist and author

You are trying not only to reach your potential but move beyond it. If you are not in the best shape you can be, these things simply become more difficult to achieve.

Rick Pitino, basketball coach

Turn off your mind, relax and float down stream.

George Harrison, the Beatles

Eat breakfast like a king, lunch like a prince and dinner like a pauper.

Dana Martin, fitness expert

You've got to be in top physical condition. Fatigue makes cowards of us all.

Vince Lombardi, football coach

A vacation is what you take when you can't take any more of what you've been taking.

Steve Gregory, financial sales motivator

The only way to keep your health is to eat what you don't want, drink what you don't like, and do what you'd druther not.

Mark Twain, American author

Growing old can kiss my ass!

Frank Sinatra, singer and entertainer

It is exercise alone that supports the spirits, and keeps the mind in vigor.

Cicero, Roman philosopher

Tell me what you eat and I will tell you who you are.

Anthelme Brillat-Savarin, French lawyer and politician

The glutton digs his grave with his teeth.

Old English saying

Always rise from the table with an appetite, and you will never sit down without one.

William Penn, founder of Pennsylvania

For the sake of health, medicines are taken by weight and measure; so ought food to be, or by some similar rule.

John Skelton, English poet

The stomach is a slave that must accept everything that is given to it, but which avenges wrongs as slyly as does the slave.

Emile Souvestre, French novelist

Fresh air impoverishes the doctor.

Danish saying

Take rest; a field that has rested gives a bountiful crop.

Ovid, poet

If I knew I was going to live this long, I'd have taken better care of myself.

Mickey Mantle, baseball player

Good health and good sense are two of life's greatest blessings.

Publilius Syrus, Roman philosopher

A good laugh and a long sleep are the best cures in the doctor's book.

Irish saying

Health is the soul that animates all the enjoyments of life, which fade and are tasteless without it.

Seneca, Roman philosopher

If you have health, you probably will be happy, and if you have health and happiness, you have all the wealth you need, even if it is not all you want.

Elbert Hubbard, writer and publisher

If you don't take care of yourself, the undertaker will overtake that responsibility for you.

Carrie Latet, writer and poet

He who has health has hope; and he who has hope has everything.

Thomas Carlyle, Scottish writer and historian

It is health that is real wealth and not pieces of gold and silver.

Mahatma Gandhi, spiritual and political leader of India

I take the true definition of exercise to be labor without weariness.

Samuel Johnson, English author and journalist.

To enjoy good health, to bring true happiness to one's family, to bring peace to all, one must first discipline and control one's own mind. If a man can control his mind he can find the way to Enlightenment, and all wisdom and virtue will naturally come to him.

Buddha, founder of Buddhism

The secret of health for both mind and body is not to mourn for the past, worry about the future, or anticipate troubles, but to live in the present moment wisely and earnestly.

Buddha, founder of Buddhism

Every human being is the author of his own health or disease.

Buddha, founder of Buddhism

To keep the body in good health is a duty . . . otherwise we shall not be able to keep our mind strong and clear.

Buddha, founder of Buddhism

Health is the greatest possession. Contentment is the greatest treasure. Confidence is the greatest friend. Non-being is the greatest joy.

Lao Tzu, founder of Taoism

A man's health can be judged by which he takes two at a time—pills or stairs.

Joan Welsh

Walking is the best possible exercise. Habituate yourself to walk very far.

U.S. President Thomas Jefferson

Health is worth more than learning.

> U.S. President Thomas Jefferson

A strong body makes the mind strong.

> U.S. President Thomas Jefferson

The alimentary canal is thirty-two feet long. You control only the first three inches of it. Control it well.

> Kin Hubbard, cartoonist and journalist

Diet cures more than the lancet.

> Spanish proverb

One meal a day is enough for a lion, and it ought to suffice for a man.

> Dr. George Fordyce, Scottish physician and lecturer

Many dishes bring many diseases.

> Pliny the Elder, author and philosopher

There are many troubles which you cannot cure by the Bible and the hymn-book, but which you can cure by a good perspiration and a breath of fresh air.

> Henry Ward Beecher, clergyman and abolitionist

Action is the antidote to despair.

> Joan Baez, musician

The rule is simple: Be sober and temperate, and you will be healthy.

> Benjamin Franklin, statesman

The firefly only shines when on the wing; so is it with the mind; when once we rest, we darken.

> Philip James Bailey, English poet

The destiny of nations depends upon the manner in which they feed themselves.

> Anthelme Brillat-Savarin, French lawyer and politician

Subdue your appetites, my dears, and you've conquered human nature.

Charles Dickens, English novelist

All philosophy lies in two words, sustain and abstain.

Epictetus, Greek philosopher

I dressed and went for a walk—determined not to return until I took in what Nature had to offer.

Raymond Carver, short story writer and poet

Walking is man's best medicine.

Hippocrates, Greek physician and the Father of Medicine

Sometimes the most urgent thing you can possibly do is take a complete rest.

Ashleigh Brilliant, cartoonist

Rest is the sweet sauce of labor.

Plutarch, Roman historian

Chapter 28

Reward Yourself Regularly and Often

Life is too short to drink the house wine.
> Helen Thomas, reporter and White House Press correspondent

If people concentrated on the really important things in life, there'd be a shortage of fishing poles.
> Doug Larson, British Olympian

If a man insisted always on being serious and never allowed himself a bit of fun and relaxation, he would go mad or become unstable without knowing it.
> Herodotus, Greek historian

Men for the sake of getting a living forget to live.
> Margaret Fuller, journalist and activist

Take rest; a field that has rested gives a bountiful crop.
> Ovid, Roman poet

Loafing needs no explanation and is its own excuse.
> Christopher Morley, journalist and novelist

Half our life is spent trying to find something to do with the time we have rushed through life trying to save.
> Will Rogers, humorist and comedian

Take time to smell the roses.
> Russian Proverb

Stress is nothing more than a socially acceptable form of mental illness.
> Richard Carlson, author and psychotherapist

Almost all creativity involves purposeful play.
Abraham Maslow, psychologist

No matter how much pressure you feel at work, if you could find ways to relax for at least five minutes every hour, you'd be more productive.
Dr Joyce Brothers, psychologist and advice columnist

All work and no play makes Jack a dull boy and Jill a rich widow.
Evan Esar, American humorist

Time spent laughing is time spent with the gods.
Japanese proverb

This art of resting the mind and the power of dismissing from it all care and worry is probably one of the secrets of energy in our great men.
Captain J.A. Hadfield

Have fun even if it kills you!
Howell Norfolk

And we should consider every day lost on which we have not danced at least once.
Friedrich Nietzsche, German philosopher

The rule of my life is to make business a pleasure, and pleasure my business.
Aaron Burr Jr., American Revolutionary War hero

Time you enjoyed wasting is not wasted time.
T. S. Elliot, author

The secret to a rewarding life: Something to do, something to look forward to and someone to love.
Author unknown

There is no duty we so much underrate as the duty of being happy.
Robert Louis Stevenson, Scottish novelist and poet

The greatest of all pleasures is to give pleasure to one whom we love.
Stanislas de Boufflers, French statesman and writer

Man is most nearly himself when he achieves the seriousness of a child at play.
Heraclitus, Greek philosopher

Give me golf clubs, fresh air and a beautiful partner and you can keep the golf clubs and the fresh air.
Jack Benny, comedian

Laughter is an instant vacation.
Milton Berle, comedian

People rarely succeed unless they have fun in what they are doing.
Dale Carnegie, success trainer and author

Without adventure civilization is in full decay.
Alfred North Whitehead, mathematician and philosopher

Too much of a good thing is wonderful.
May West, actress

He who does not get fun and enjoyment out of every day . . . needs to reorganize his life.
George Matthew Adams

He enjoys true leisure who has time to improve his soul's estate.
Henry David Thoreau, writer and philosopher

One must be out-of-doors enough to get experience of wholesome reality, as a ballast to thought and sentiment. Health requires this relaxation, this aimless life.
Henry David Thoreau, writer and philosopher

When you can not get a compliment in any other way, pay yourself one.
Mark Twain, American author

One of the symptoms of an approaching nervous breakdown is the belief that one's work is terribly important.
Bertrand Russell, British philosopher

Next to the virtue, the fun in this world is what we can least spare.
Agnes Strickland, English writer and poet

There is more to life than increasing its speed.
Mahatma Gandhi, spiritual and political leader of India

Sometimes I sits and thinks and sometimes I just sits.
Satchel Paige, baseball player

I feel that the greatest reward for doing is the opportunity to do more.
Dr. Jonas Salk, biologist and physician

The shortest pleasures are the sweetest.
George Farquhar, Irish writer and playwright

Life must be lived as play
Plato, Greek philosopher

Sometimes the cure for restlessness is rest.
Colleen Wainwright, writer

Take time every day to do something silly.
Philips Walker

The biggest reward for a thing well done is to have done it.
Voltaire, French writer and philosopher

Find what brings you joy and go there.
Jan Phillips, author and speaker

Slow down and everything you are chasing will come around and catch you.
John De Paola

For fast acting relief . . . try slowing down.

Lily Tomlin, comedian and actress

Just keep taking chances and having fun.

Garth Brooks, musician

The man who doesn't relax and hoot a few hoots voluntarily, now and then, is in great danger of hooting hoots and standing on his head for the edification of the pathologist and trained nurse, a little later on.

Elbert Hubbard, writer and publisher

A cheerful frame of mind, reinforced by relaxation is the medicine that puts all ghosts of fear on the run.

George Matthew Adams, columnist

Unless you choose to do great things with it, it makes no difference how much you are rewarded.

Oprah Winfrey, actress and media mogul

Chapter 29

The Winning Sales Attitude and Mindset!

Get ready for some miracles baby!
Jim Valvano, basketball coach

Your altitude is determined by your attitude.
Author unknown

Go hard or go home!
Speedo advertisement

You don't have to be the biggest to beat the biggest.
H. Ross Perot, billionaire

I am an optimist. It does not seem too much use being anything else.
Sir Winston Churchill, British Prime Minister

Believing you can do it goes a long way.
Michael Phelps, U.S. Olympian

To achieve great things we must live as though we were never going to die.
Luc de Clapiers, French writer

The words you consistently select will shape your destiny.
Anthony Robbins, success trainer and author

Some people freeze to death in the winter, other people ski.
Anthony Robbins, success trainer and author

It is not your aptitude, but your attitude, that determines your altitude.
Zig Ziglar, sales trainer

If you think you can or you can't . . . you're right!
Zig Ziglar, motivational and sales author

Great fear will always lose out to great faith.
Zig Ziglar, motivational and sales author

You are so much better than you know.
Sade, singer and songwriter

Give me a museum and I'll fill it!
Pablo Picasso, artist

You've tried all the rest, now try the best.
Motto on Ray's Pizza boxes

The secret to happiness is to count your blessings while others are adding up their troubles.
William Penn, founding father of Pennsylvania

Who has confidence in himself will gain the confidence of others.
Leib Lazarow, author

The greatest lesson of life is that you are responsible for your life.
Oprah Winfrey, actress and media mogul

It is a fabulous country, the only fabulous country; it is the only place where miracles not only happen, but where they happen all the time.
Tom Wolfe, author

The question isn't at what age I want to retire; it's at what income.
George Foreman, boxer

Success in life is 95% mental; the other 5% is in your head.
Yogi Berra, baseball coach and player

The mind is its own place, and in itself, can make a heaven of hell, and a hell of heaven.
John Milton, English poet

When I call on a client, I come by cab and I am sleek and clean and foursquare. I carry myself as though I've made a quiet killing on the stock market and have come to call more as a public service than anything else.

Kurt Vonnegut, from *Welcome to the Monkey House*

You must be the change you wish to see in the world.

Mahatma Gandhi, political and spiritual leader of India

Make a dent in the universe.

Steve Jobs, founder of Apple Computer

We who lived in concentration camps can remember the men who walked through the huts comforting others, giving away their last piece of bread. They may have been few in number, but they offer sufficient proof that everything can be taken from a man but one thing: the last of human freedoms—to choose one's attitude in any given set of circumstances—to choose one's own way.

Victor Frankl, Holocaust survivor

They who lost today may win tomorrow.

Miguel de Cervantes, Spanish novelist

Discounting of fees and commissions is a sign of poor self-esteem.

Kevin Dyerly, financial advisor

The good news is the bad news can be turned into good news when you change your attitude.

Dr. Robert Schuller, spiritual leader

If it's going to be, it's up to me.

Dr. Robert Schuller, spiritual leader

God's delays are not God's denials.

Dr. Robert Schuller, spiritual leader

When you win, nothing hurts.

Joe Namath, football player

Say you are well, or all is well with you, and God shall hear your words and make them come true.
Ella Wheeler Wilcox, poet and writer

They can do all . . . because they think they can.
Virgil, Roman poet

Ability is what you're capable of doing. Motivation determines what you do. Attitude determines how well you do it.
Lou Holtz, football coach

Success comes in cans, not cants.
Brian Tracy, sales trainer

I don't run a race to see who's the fastest, I run to see who has the most guts.
Steve "Pre" Prefontaine, runner

When I do good, I feel good. When I do bad, I feel bad, and that's my religion.
U.S. President Abraham Lincoln

Most of us are about as happy as we make up our minds to be.
U.S. President Abraham Lincoln

Having a healthier, more alive, passionate, creative, and empowered life is a fantasy that I choose for myself. I, for one, believe that all of creation is sacred. I want to believe in the tooth fairy, the sandman, the Easter bunny, Santa Claus, leprechauns, unicorns, and all the other magical beings that help bridge the gap between the possible and impossible. When I look at the faces of children who believe in such magical beings, I see the sense of wonder and awe in their eyes. Identifying with these magical beings may lead, in time, to frustration and even despair, but identification with the possibilities of the unseen magic they represent is the basis for all hope, religious story, and all healing.
Donald M. Epstein, *Healing Myths, Healing Magic*

You gotta believe!
Tug McGraw, relief pitcher

The happy ending is our country's national belief.

Mary McCarthy, author and critic

You don't get to choose how you are going to die. Or when. You can only decide how you're going to live—Now!

Joan Baez, musician

The optimist claims we live in the best of all possible worlds, and the pessimist fears this is true.

U.S. President John Adams

Good manners are made up of petty sacrifices.

Ralph Waldo Emerson, philosopher

People seem not to see that their opinion of the world is also a confession of character.

Ralph Waldo Emerson, philosopher

Every man is entitled to be valued by his best moment.

Ralph Waldo Emerson, philosopher

There is no beautifier of complexion or form to scatter joy and not pain around us.

Ralph Waldo Emerson, philosopher

To me, old age is always 15 years older than I am.

Bernard Baruch, financier and presidential advisor

Some people are always grumbling because roses have thorns. I am thankful that thorns have roses.

Alphonse Karr, novelist

Half this game is 90% mental.

Yogi Berra, baseball manager and player

If you think an expert is expensive, wait until you hire an amateur.

Red Adair, oil well firefighter

Do not let what you cannot do interfere with what you can do.
John Wooden, basketball coach

Too many people overvalue what they are not and undervalue what they are.
Malcolm Forbes, publisher

If you want to be respected by others, the great thing is to respect yourself.
Fyodor Dostoyevsky, novelist

What we must decide is how we are valuable, rather than how valuable we are.
F. Scott Fitzgerald, writer

Whether you think you can or that you can't, you are usually right.
Henry Ford, automotive titan

Hate less, love more and all good things are yours.
Swedish proverb

Any fool can criticize, condemn and complain . . . and most fools do.
Dale Carnegie, success trainer and author

I've never been poor, only broke. Being poor is a frame of mind. Being broke is only a temporary situation.
Mike Todd, film producer

You can do very little with faith, but you can do nothing without it.
Samuel Butler, author and poet

It is what it is.
Zen saying

To succeed, it is necessary to accept the world as it is and rise above it.
Michael Korda, novelist and publishing editor

What is a cynic? A man who knows the price of everything and the value of nothing.

Oscar Wilde, Irish playwright and poet

We are all in the gutter, but some of us are looking at the stars.

Oscar Wilde, Irish playwright and poet

It is not well for a man to pray cream and live skim milk.

Henry Ward Beecher, clergyman and abolitionist

Positive belief at the start of a doubtful undertaking is often the one thing ensuring its successful outcome.

William James, psychologist and philosopher

The greatest discovery of my generation is that a human being can alter his life by altering his attitude.

William James, psychologist, psychologist and philosopher

Pessimism leads to weakness, optimism to power.

William James, psychologist and philosopher

The sun's gonna shine and the rain's gonna fall, and in the end you might get burnt or wet, but that's life. So dance in the puddles and bathe in the sun and at the end of the day, smile. Everything is gonna be alright.

Author unknown

Being successful in business isn't a matter of taking advantage of people who need your products and services. On the contrary, it is a matter of giving them so much value, care and attention they would feel guilty ever thinking about doing business with somebody else.

Mary Kay Ash, cosmetic titan

Five of the best things to say: I'm sorry. Thank You. Well done. You were right. Tell me about you.

Author unknown

A credo for positive people:
1. Purpose: Something to strive for. There is no right way to do the a wrong thing. There is no pillow as soft as a clear conscience.
2. Pride: People with humility don't think less of themselves; they just think about themselves less.
3. Patience: Nice guys may finish last, but usually they're running in a different race. The secret is finding something else to do in the meantime.
4. Persistence: Trying is just a noisy way of NOT doing something.
5. Perspective: Let's not imitate others. Let's find ourselves and be ourselves.

> Ted Owen

You look marvelous!

> Billy Crystal, comedian and actor

A will finds a way.

> Orison Swett Marden

I'd like to live like a poor man with lots of money.

> Pablo Picasso, painter

The thing always happens that you really believe in; and the belief in a thing makes it happen.

> Frank Lloyd Wright, architect

If you play to win, as I do, the game never ends.

> Stan Mikita, hockey player

Every great batter works on the theory that the pitcher is more afraid of him than he is of the pitcher.

> Ty Cobb, baseball player

No great performance ever came from holding back.

> Don Greene, motivational coach

So what if they're taller; we'll play big!

> George Ireland, basketball coach

Gumption: 1. Initiative, aggressiveness, resourcefulness, 2. Courage, spunk, guts

Dictionary definition

Victory is doing the best you can, and even if you lose, you will have learned something.

Bill Bowerman, co-founder of the NIKE Corporation

Here is my formula for a better attitude: Face fears, confront worries, anticipate the future.

Dr. Norman Vincent Peale, spiritual leader

Empty pockets never held anyone back. Only empty heads and empty hearts can do that.

Dr. Norman Vincent Peale, spiritual leader

Any fact facing us is not as important as our attitude toward it, for it, for that determines our success or failure.

Dr. Norman Vincent Peale, spiritual leader

We tend to get what we expect!

Dr. Norman Vincent Peale, spiritual leader

I hate to lose more than I like to win. I hate to see the happiness on their faces when they beat me.

Jimmy Connors, tennis champion

Some may try and tell us that this is the end of an era. But what they overlook is that in America, every day is a new beginning; for this is the land that has never become, but is always in the act of becoming.

U.S. President Ronald Reagan, *The Great Communicator*

Although I may not be able to prevent the worst from happening, I am responsible for my attitude toward the inevitable misfortunes that darken life. Bad things do happen; how I respond to them defines my character and the quality of my life.

Walter Anderson, publisher

The U.S. Constitution doesn't guarantee happiness, only the pursuit of it. You have to catch up to it yourself.
Benjamin Franklin, statesman

When you were born, you cried and the world rejoiced; live your life so that when you die, the world cries and you rejoice.
Cherokee saying

There's only one real sin, and that is to persuade oneself that the second-best is anything but second best.
Doris Lessing, author

Second place is first loser!
Old sports saying

The most important single ingredient in the formula of success is knowing how to get along with people.
U.S. President Theodore Roosevelt

I'm often wrong, but never in doubt.
Ivy Baker Priest, politician

Those who stand for nothing fall for everything.
Alexander Hamilton, U.S. Secretary of The Treasury

An inexhaustible good nature is one of the most precious gifts of heaven, spreading itself like oil over the troubled sea of thought, and keeping the mind smooth and equable in the roughest weather.
Washington Irving, author and historian

In the depths of winter I finally learned there was in me an invincible summer.
Albert Camus, writer

You are never given a wish without also being given the power to make it come true. You may have to work for it, however.
Richard Bach, writer

If a man is called a street sweeper, he should sweep streets even as Michelangelo painted or Beethoven composed music or Shakespeare wrote poetry. He should sweep streets so well that all the hosts of heaven and earth will pause to say, here lived a great street sweeper who did his job well.

Martin Luther King, Jr., civil rights leader

Life is just a mirror, and what you see out there, you must first see inside of you.

Wally "Famous" Amos, cookie maker

Happiness depends upon ourselves.

Aristotle, Greek philosopher

What a man thinks of himself . . . indicates his fate.

Henry David Thoreau, author and philosopher

He is able who thinks he is able.

Buddha, founder of Buddhism

The only limit to our realization of tomorrow will be our doubts of today. Let us move forward with strong and active faith.

U.S. President Franklin D. Roosevelt

A stumbling block to the pessimist is a stepping stone to the optimist.

Eleanor Roosevelt, First Lady

There is one thing that gives radiance to everything. It is the idea of something around the corner.

G.K. Chesterton, writer

One of the things I learned the hard way was that it doesn't pay to get discouraged. Keeping busy and making optimism a way of life can restore your faith in yourself.

Lucille Ball, comedian

If you can't change your fate, change your attitude.

Amy Tan, author

Life has two rules: 1. Never quit! 2. Always remember rule number 1.

Duke Ellington, Jazz musician

Ability is what you are capable of. Motivation determines what you do. Attitude determines how well you do it.

Lou Holtz, football coach

Fear less, hope more. Eat less, chew more. Whine less, breathe more. Talk less, say more. Hate less, love more . . . and all good things are yours.

Swedish proverb

May you live all the days of your life.

Jonathan Swift, Irish writer and poet

The race doesn't always go to the fastest or the strongest man, but that's usually the way to bet.

Author unknown

History will be kind to me for I intend to write it.

Sir Winston Churchill, British Prime Minister

Live your life so that even if you lose, you will be ahead.

Will Rogers, humorist and comedian

Winning is not a sometime thing: it's an all the time thing. You don't win once in a while; you don't do the right thing once in a while; you do them right all the time. Winning is a habit. Unfortunately, so is losing.

Vince Lombardi, football coach

You got to believe in yourself. Hell, I believe I'm the best looking guy in the world and I might be right.

Sir Charles Barkley, professional basketball player

The trick is growing up without growing old.

Casey Stengel, baseball coach

Man must cease attributing his problems to his environment, and learn again to exercise his will; his personal responsibility.

Albert Schweitzer, philosopher and physician

The longer I live, the more I realize the impact of attitude on life. Attitude, to me is more important than the past, than education, than money, than circumstances, than failures, than successes, than what other people think or say or do. It is more important than appearance, giftedness or skill. It will make or break a company . . . a church . . . a home. The remarkable thing is we have a choice every day regarding the attitude we will embrace for that day. We cannot change our past, we cannot change the fact that people will act in a certain way. We cannot change the inevitable. The only thing we can do is play on the one string we have, and that is our attitude. I am convinced that life is 10 percent what happens to me and 90 percent how I react to it. And so it is with you, we are in charge of our attitudes.

Charles Swindoll, clergyman and author

Keep your face to the sunshine and you cannot see the shadows.

Helen Keller, author and activist

God created the world just like a knife and left it up to us to take it by the handle or the blade.

C.J. Langenhoven, South African novelist

Float like a butterfly and sting like a bee!

Muhammad Ali, professional boxer

I am the greatest!

Muhammad Ali, professional boxer

I keep thinking, that day-to-day, something good is about to happen!

Pete Carroll, coach of the USC Trojans

Acknowledgements

S IR ISAAC NEWTON said, "If I have seen further, it is by standing on the shoulders of giants." I would like to acknowledge some of the giant Power Sales People I have learned from, worked for, sold with, hired, trained, and managed. Their sales technique, tutelage, and own personal sales philosophies have been educational, entertaining and invaluable to me in my selling and sales management career.

In alphabetical order, thank you to Ralph Acampora, Jonno Alcaro, Dave Altshuler, Daniela Bar-Illan, Gina Batista, Warren Bischoff, Larry Birnbaum, Jeff Brown, Geoffrey Byruch, Jeff Cain, Joe Castellucio, The Chodorow Group in La Jolla, Michael Clurman, Gene Cooper, Todd Cowle, Steve Dantus, Liam Dalton, Tim Dumas, Kevin Dyerly, Bob Filderman, The Flynn Clan in Rockaway, Peter Foley, Bob Feinman, Mark Freiberg, Paul Ganun, David Garfinkle, Sonia Gladden, Richard Gleason, Craig Goldstone, Alan "Ace" Greenberg, Steve Gregory, Steve Hagendorf, Jay Harms, Ed "Herms" Herman, Tony Iati, David Janke, Wally Kaner of The Athlete's Foot, Jaci Fuchs-Kessler, Michael King, Peter Leahy, Frank and Kathy Maloney, Mike Maloney, Susan Maloney, Al "Doc" Mance, Mike "Mugsey" McGinnis, Jerry Messana, Alex Middleton, Ed Nass, Seth Novatt, Steve O'Brien, Vincent "Guy" Puma, Ragin Raven, Ash Rajan, Mike Sassano, Rich Saperstein, Clark Schubach, Bill Smith, Jay Spieler, Scott Stern, Steve Temes, Jim Venetos, Steve Viets, Peter Wagner and John "Q" Wells.

Thank you to Gerry Counihan for his upbeat attitude and wonderful advice for the cover art.

Most importantly, thank you to my wife Anna and our beautiful and energetic daughter, Wynn. Wynn has taught us what real selling is about since the day she was born—when you're out of ways to ask for the order, just keep asking over and over, again and again, until you get what you want!

About the Author

C HRISTOPHER J. MALONEY has over 25 years of experience in financial sales, sales training, sales management and investment banking on Wall Street. In 1983 he started his selling career in New York City at the age of 19 and became an Account Executive with BearStearns and Company in 1985. Chris has held numerous management positions with several top-tier Wall Street investment banking firms and rose to the positions of West Coast Regional Sales Manager and Branch Manager for a major investment firm in La Jolla, California. In 2001 he became National Sales Manager for a leading investment banking firm in New York City.

Chris has been involved with the recruiting and training of thousands of Financial Advisors during his tenure as a sales trainer with a nationally known investment banking firm. He has had the privilege to sell with, hire, recruit, train and manage some of the highest producing commission sales people in the world. During his career, he has also lived in Phoenix and Scottsdale Arizona as well as La Jolla, California. Currently, Chris is a Managing Director with a boutique investment banking firm in New York City. Chris specializes in meeting the corporate financing needs of private and publicly traded healthcare and consumer products companies.

Chris attended Embry Riddle Aeronautical University and graduated from Pace University in New York City with a Bachelor of Business Administration in 1989. He has been on the advisory boards of several private companies and is a member of The Market Technicians Association. Chris is Series 7, 63, 9 and 10 Registered with the Financial Industry Regulatory Authority (FINRA) and also has a New York State Real Estate Salesperson License. Chris is a certified Swimming Official with Metro Swimming in New York City and is also a member of The New York Athletic Club.

Contact the author at *PowerQuotes@AOL.com*